Strategic Issues in
Information Technology

Strategic Issues in Information Technology

International implications for decision makers

Edited by Professor Hellmut Schütte
Director, Euro-Asia Centre, INSEAD, France

Published by Pergamon Infotech Ltd,
Maidenhead, Berkshire, England.

Typeset by First Page Ltd, Watford, Hertfordshire, England.

Printed in Great Britain by A. Wheaton & Co. Ltd, Exeter, England.

British Library Cataloguing in Publication Data
Strategic issues in information technology:
international implications for decision makers.
1. Information systems – For management
I. Schütte, Hellmut
001.5

ISBN 0-08-036517-5

Contents

List Of Contributors

Warren Earl Davis
Vice President, American Semiconductor Association, US.

Chris Freeman
Emeritus Professor, University of Sussex, UK.

Tage Frisk
Vice President, R&D, IBM Europe.

Youichi Ito
Professor, Keio University, Japan.

Koji Kobayashi
Chairman, NEC, Japan.

Adrian Norman
Senior Consultant, Arthur D Little, UK.

Kazuo Ogura
Deputy Director General, Economic Affairs Bureau,
Japanese Ministry of Foreign Affairs, Japan.

Jonathon Parapak
President, Indosat, Indonesia.

Peter Robinson
Special Advisor, International Infomatics, Canadian
Department of Communications, Canada.

Hellmut Schütte
Director, Euro-Asia Centre, Insead, France.

Su Shaozhi
Professor, Chinese Academy of Sciences.

Louis Turner
Director, International Business and Technology
Programme, Royal Institute of International Affairs. UK.

Introduction

The framework

Of all the technical changes that have influenced our lives in recent years, it is those in information technology which have had the greatest impact. They will continue to do so at least until the end of the century, when other major technological breakthroughs in the area of new materials, biotechnology or energy may force entirely new ways of living on humankind.

The development of information technology has been spectacular, first in the output of new components, computers, and communication equipment and systems which have been brought on to the market, and secondly in the realm of users, who are finding an increasing number of applications for these new technologies. By integrating information technology into factories, offices, etc, productivity is increased and capabilities multiplied. This creates a basis for further demand and accelerates the search for even more advanced technology.

In a world concerned with the limits of growth, it seems that information technology represents an area of potentially limitless growth. In fact, with regard to technological progress as well as the diffusion of technology, the world may have seen only the beginning of the information technology era, or just the bare emergence of a new society which calls itself an information society. This holds true for developing countries, but it even applies to the most technologically advanced countries.

While the advent of technological progress is undeniable, negative side-effects have become apparent. Growing inequalities between nations, companies and individuals can be observed. Growing friction between these groups is emerging, and there is a general feeling of uneasiness about the future — be it with regard to one's own cultural identity or to questions of long-term employment opportunities.

There are two explanations for these trends. First, because of the speed of change, it is less possible to take guidelines from the past and apply them to the future. Experience has lost some of its value. What is needed today is continual learning and complete openness towards new developments. An active management of change is becoming crucial.

Second, impacts of information technology are not limited to a geographically or politically defined area. The production and distribution of information — the ultimate objective of all activities in the information technology sector — does not recognise any borders. Government control is limited, and will probably diminish even further as the world comes closer to being a global village. Greater interdependence means that policy makers cannot take decisions based purely on national criteria. Almost all major policy changes have an impact on other countries; similarly, decisions taken abroad influence domestic affairs. Thus, the technological and economic dimensions of information technology have become international. The political dimension, however, remains largely nationally oriented.

Today, this discrepancy represents a major stumbling block to further progress in information technology. Many of the issues can no longer be solved unilaterally and need international coordination. The multinational firms are very involved and are the best suited to overcome national constraints. However, they may not be the best guarantors of the welfare of the world's people. The mission of political decision makers is to take care of the interests of their local or national constituencies, but they are not necessarily concerned with the international dimension of the issues raised.

The international electronic mailbox, teleconferences which bridge continents, or access to databases worldwide, will remain gadgets or superficial proof of a globalisation process, if not accompanied by a change in the attitudes of decision makers towards a common goal. Change will require time, effort and a view of the world as parts of a whole, rather than as a whole divided into parts.

Content of the book

To foster international understanding, and to contribute to the progress of smoother and better international decision making in information technology, in 1985 the Japanese Government launched a major project called TIDE 2000. It attempted to generate knowledge and an exchange of views on the broader impact of information technology in the international arena. TIDE 2000 brought together senior government officials, business leaders and academics from all over the world; their first meeting was in Tokyo, followed by a second in Honolulu, and by a final meeting in 1987 at INSEAD's Euro-Asia Centre in Fontainebleau (France).

This book draws heavily, but not exclusively, on papers presented and discussed during the Fontainebleau conference. As such, the contributions contained in this volume do not reproduce the conference proceedings which have been compiled elsewhere.

The authors in this publication come from Europe, Japan, North America, China and Indonesia. They are either part of industry, observers of it, or are concerned with decision making in information technology at the political level. Their views do not necessarily represent those held by the organisations with which they are or have been connected.

In Part I of this book, 'Forecasting the Information Technology Evolution' is discussed. Koji Kobayashi and Tage Frisk outline future developments and their implications for society and decision makers. Koji Kobayashi focuses on the potential uses for integrated systems data networks — C&C systems — while Tage Frisk discusses technological advancements in each of the implicated industries — computers, semiconductors, telecommunications and software.

Part II outlines 'The Limits of Policy Making in Information Technology'. Kazuo Ogura describes the conflict which exists between domestically oriented government policies and the internationally focused objectives of commerce and industry. Peter Robinson points out that decision making in international organisations is not an easy task; there are no general guidelines to follow and no dedicated international forum in which such guidelines can be discussed and defined.

Part III explores issues connected with 'International Competition and Collaboration in Information Technology'. Louis Turner describes the state of competition between the US, Europe and Japan, noting the loss of strength in Europe and the weakening of the US, but, at the same time, questioning the ability of the Japanese to lead. Warren Davis stresses that free competition must be fair competition, especially in industries of vital importance to countries' future economic potential.

Finally, the driving forces behind international alliances in information technology, and the implications for policy makers attempting to control or support them, are analysed by Adrian Norman.

Part IV looks at 'Information Technology and Developing Countries'. The authors consider information technology as both a threat and an opportunity for developing countries. Shaozhi Su elaborates on some of those threats and, at the same time, sees some of the positive sides to the growing use of information technologies. Jonathan Parapak from Indonesia reports on his country's progress in telecommunications and discusses the implications for economic, cultural and political life.

Part V concentrates on 'Information Technology and the Individual'. Youicho Ito points out that better communication facilities have improved opportunities for learning from other cultures, but that foreign influences can become overpowering. He then examines what makes some countries more easily overwhelmed by foreign cultures than others. Hellmut Schütte looks at the replacement of human labour through new technologies and argues that the real challenge for policy makers does not lie in financing people who are out of work, but in giving the unemployed an equal and respected position in society.

Part VI provides conceptual ideas on 'Information Technology and the New Economic Paradigm'. Chris Freeman considers that the developments in computers will lead to a change in the economic paradigm. Before the full potentiality of the new paradigm can be realised, major organisational, managerial and social, as well as economic, adaptations will be required. Changes of this magnitude will take time and, thus, the industrialised world may be only at the very beginning of what will be a long, painful period of readjustment.

A biographical note on each author follows their paper.

Acknowledgements

The driving force behind the TIDE 2000 project was Mr Kazuo Ogura, at that time Minister at the Japanese Delegation to the Organisation for Economic Cooperation and Development (OECD) — a man with an open mind, broad interests and a keen awareness of the opportunities and constraints of international cooperation. Although his direct involvement in the production of this book was limited to his paper, he has, nevertheless, influenced me sufficiently to set about the task of making the thoughts of the authors known to a wider audience.

To these authors, I am greatly indebted. For most of them, writing is not their main concern and had to be done in addition to their normal, heavy workloads. The diligence of some of the authors in responding to requests for additional comments on the topics was highly appreciated.

Finally, the volume would not have been produced without the tremendous efforts of Mrs Michele Jurgens-Panak, an American graduate of INSEAD, who carried the editing work forward despite my frequent absences from Fontainebleau.

To all of them, I would like to express my gratitude.

Hellmut Schütte, Editor
Fontainebleau, France
1988

PART I

Forecasting the Information Technology Evolution

Technological innovation is at the heart of the information technology revolution and none of what we have experienced, or will experience, could be possible without it. Society should not take innovation for granted. A few years ago, the sector which is now called information technology was limited to data processing. The step from this very limited function to that of being a centre of human activity is a substantial one. The change from information management to knowledge production is the next, big step, not only requiring the convergence of computers and communication systems, but also requiring major investments in software development.

The two following authors provide some insight into the chances for success in the future and indicate some of the bottlenecks to development. Koji Kobayashi elaborates on the integration of computers and communication systems, but cautions that much work has yet to be done in the area of software development. He believes that advancement towards an automated interpretation communication system should be promoted in order to achieve real international communication.

Future progress in hardware depends heavily on developments in related technological fields, as argued by Tage Frisk who, however, expects a continuation of major breakthroughs over the coming years.

To benefit from advancements in technology and in future international media, standards need to be set and agreed upon among firms and governments; efforts must be undertaken by those involved to spread the new innovations as widely as possible and to the advantage of all.

Information and Communications Technology: A Look at the Future

Koji Kobayashi

One of the outstanding characteristics of the information revolution is the way in which three separate technologies — communication, computer and semiconductor — have combined to form the foundation of a fourth which is more than a technology and even more pervasive than an industry. With practically limitless growth potential, the information technology phenomenon today encompasses all of its three parent technologies and will soon involve or impact all other industries, our economies as a whole, and the entirety of our societies, cultures and futures.

Information technology has its technological foundation in the communication, computer and semiconductor sciences. The objective of this paper is to provide an overview of the major developments in these three sectors and to indicate what we might expect in the future on the basis of present trends in these technologies and their related industries. Information and communication systems will be discussed in two areas — in manufacturing and in the home. The various effects information technologies are likely to have on society — specifically on employment and cultural identity — will also be considered.

This paper will also touch upon the element of international cooperation, which is desperately needed to ensure transfer of technology and the provision of training for developing countries, and to permit the creation of worldwide information and communication systems. Finally, the author will comment on the expected role of the Centre for Telecommunications Development.

Past developments and future trends

In the author's speech at INTELCOM 77 in Atlanta, Georgia in 1977, the concept of an information technology based on the integration of computer and communications technologies was first presented. A year later, speaking to the 3rd US-Japan Computer Conference in San Francisco, the author coined a phrase for the phenomenon, calling it 'C&C' — standing for the Integration of Computers and Communications.

Parallel developments in telecommunications, computers and semiconductors are rapidly making C&C a reality. In communications, digital technology is being introduced worldwide in most major communication systems for both transmission and switching. Such technology allows all types of communication media — voice, data, image and video — to be passed simultaneously to wherever digital networks exist to receive them. With digital technology as a common basis, the integration of world communication systems is an immediate possibility. Today, this integration is already being sought by such bodies as the International Telegraph and Telephone Consultative Committee of the International Telecommunication Union (CCITT), which is advocating worldwide standardisation under the Integrated Services Digital Network system, or ISDN as it is commonly known.

In the computer industry, progress in design and construction techniques has followed a path from single-function type computers, to multifunctional computers, then to large-scale centralised processing units and to very powerful units able to perform extensive distribution processing and networking. The next step will be towards intelligent processing using artificial intelligence.

Like computers, progress in semiconductors has been rapid, moving from transistors, to integrated circuits, to large-scale integrated circuits, and now to very large-scale integrated circuits. Microscopic-size chips will soon have the capability to out-perform the huge computers of the early 1970s.

It is important to note that the latest two advancements in the arena of computers — distribution processing and networking — would not have been possible without the earlier developments in telecommunications which allowed independent terminals and mainframe computers to be connected through communication lines using digital technology.

At an even more basic level, advancements in semiconductor technology have been a condition for the development of computer and communications technologies.

It is the rapid and interrelated technological advancements in these three sectors that are making information technology not just another growing industry but a phenomenon. We are only now realising the extent to which these developments enhance one another and increase the possible applications of information technologies in the future.

It is the author's belief that continued development in semiconductor and digital technologies will soon lead to the full-scale integration of computers and communications, and that in the coming century these C&C systems will play an increasingly important role in our social, economic and political infrastructures.

Future information and communications systems

If we consider the immense and unforeseen leaps humankind has made in the information technology field in the last 20 years, then we might hesitate to make forecasts about which developments will dominate over the next 20 years; C&C systems at the turn of the century may be very different from those on which we are working today. Still, it can be useful to extrapolate into the future using the present trends in technological developments for C&C systems. Such a look at the future may even help us to define our present goals more clearly.

Major changes as a result of C&Cs are expected in two principal areas — in manufacturing and in the home.

FUTURE MANUFACTURING SYSTEMS

With a higher all-round level of education and a better quality of life, the material needs of the general public will be more complex and sophisticated. A wide variety of products tailored to the individual's requirements will have to be manufactured in small quantities and thus with high efficiency.

The more 'intelligent' or complex the product, the more knowledge-intensive its manufacture will be. Each product will require a high degree of input from immediately available data centres relying on sophisticated software. Thus, in the final product, the information 'content' will be much greater than it is today and will thereby comprise a more significant amount of the total production cost.

To provide an example of how future C&C systems might operate, imagine a customer's product requirements and specifications going via communications circuits directly to the company's design centre. Here, the information is processed and then used to formulate the instructions required for production. These are in turn sent by internal computer communication to the manufacturing plant nearest to the customer; the product is produced according to specifications and delivered.

Such a production process requires man/machine interactive Computer-aided Design (CAD) at the product design stage; Computer-aided Manufacturing (CAM) using computers and robots to handle process/assembly and testing at the production plant; and Computer-aided Maintenance Service (CAMS) which will rely on a database of customer and product information to provide rapid and efficient after-sale service to customers.

Customers, design centres with technical information processing systems, production plants, maintenance service centres located close to major markets, control centres with control information processing systems — all of which are geographically dispersed — will be integrated by C&C.

With each function integrated in a network, this C&C manufacturing system will be able to rapidly make and service products exactly suited to the individual customer's needs, at both higher quality and lower cost.

The creation of an individual response design system, capable of handling personalised orders flexibly, would be the next logical, technological step. Such a system would handle not just orders with design specifications, but orders consisting only of customers' conceptual demands. From the concept it would create the product specifications and manufacturing instructions; it would thus be a complete creative design system.

Eventually, we can even envisage a plant where the customers themselves control the entire manufacturing process — from submitting their design concept to receiving the finished products. Resource-sharing systems would also be feasible, in which production facilities and materials could be effectively shared among plants and enterprises dispersed throughout the entire world.

FUTURE HOME SYSTEMS

With the increase in leisure time and the diversification of life-styles, entertainment will become more individualised. In the home, entertainment will focus on the home computer/communication system. The home system of the future will be equipped to meet a wide variety of family needs, be they educational or recreational.

In terms of technical enhancements, there will be greater programme selection and increased reception time. Video and audio quality will be enhanced with high-definition television, larger screens and three-dimensional sound systems. Such improvements will lead to increased viewer satisfaction, especially in the live coverage of sports events or concerts.

Home systems will be able to take advantage of the greater availability of packaged information, for example, on laser disks which will be used to record not only movies and music, but also encyclopaedias, dictionaries and teaching materials.

Live television and radio services will continue to operate alongside the newer videotext and teletext services which will provide news, weather forecasts, regional information and news of financial market conditions. The more detailed information we now obtain from magazines and newspapers will be available on request from the electronic media.

At home and in one's own time, it will be possible to shop, make bank transactions, settle administrative affairs, make hotel, travel or theatre reservations, and even consult the doctor.

Telecommuting will become a reality as the Integrated Services Digital Network (ISDN) makes possible the individual use of wide-band communication circuits. Once society adjusts to the new environment, people will begin to take advantage of the possibilities to cut commuting time and reduce transportation and energy costs. Moreover, with many people working from home or 'travelling' via videophones, living patterns will be liberalised; employment opportunities for homemakers, the aged and the physically handicapped will expand.

One can also forecast an increase in productivity as people are released from time constraints and thus able to work during their most efficient time of day. In creative jobs, the effects will be particularly pronounced, and mothers with young children will find that child care and work become compatible.

By just looking at some of the many changes in the home and in manufacturing that may come about in the future, we can see that our lives are likely to become very different. The transition from today's society and economic structure to that of the future will be difficult, and will demand a large degree of flexibility. Such a transition will certainly pose problems, and society will undergo many changes, some of which are already being experienced today.

Two areas where we can already see dramatic changes occurring are employment and cultural identity.

The impact of information technology on employment

Rapid progress is being made in the automation of production in primary and secondary industries, and office automation will soon become widespread in the secondary and tertiary industries. This will lead to reductions in conventional jobs in farming, factories and offices. Society will have difficulty reabsorbing this redundant labour and sectorial unemployment will pose a significant political and economic problem for the industrialised nations.

Fortunately, information technologies will also create new jobs. In two areas — the software and service sectors of tertiary industry — the gains are expected to be considerable.

THE SOFTWARE INDUSTRY

The importance of software to the functioning and growth of information technology is now being recognised. Corporate managers are realising that they must anticipate investing much more in software. In production, hardware costs are steadily dropping whereas software costs are growing and form an increasing percentage of the cost of an integrated product.

Software is vital to all computer operations and the demand for it can only increase. As C&C systems are introduced throughout society, there will be a huge demand for software. This demand can only be met if the percentage of the population engaged in software production grows accordingly. It is, thus, into these jobs that the surplus labour from the 'sunset' industries must be directed. In the long run, the industry of software creation, adaptation and application will become a major employer.

Today, the rapidly growing demand for software is already evident. As microcomputers with large-scale integration have become available, they are being used for an ever greater number of applications and range of equipment and systems; home-heating and cooling equipment, microwave ovens, video-cassette recorders, compact-disk players, telephones and cars all use microcomputers and require function-specific software to make them work.

Communication equipment and networks also have a growing number of software needs as they begin to incorporate information processing functions and become intelligent. The largest growth areas for software in communications are in electronic switching systems, value-added networks, and network operation, administration and maintenance.

Expanded software use is not limited to new technologies. There are also many existing computer systems which are technically able to perform a greater number of tasks than they do at present. New or updated software, which allows these systems to perform the new tasks and to be more user friendly in present tasks, would find immediate market applicability.

The present concern of most industry observers is that the growth in demand for software is being met with a lack of supply, and the gap between demand and supply is growing rapidly. Software supply depends almost entirely upon the availability of trained software specialists, of which there are relatively few due to the newness of the field and to the lack of training or retraining facilities. As it will take some time before the necessary infrastructure is in place, we can assume that a quick solution to the present shortage is unlikely. We could even say that there is a 'software crisis'.

In order to avoid serious difficulties in the information technology industry as a result of the software crisis, a minimum of preventive steps must be taken. Societies can start by encouraging surplus labour to retrain and enter software production. Another measure would be to provide incentives to suitably skilled workers to change jobs. Short of such changes, society risks hampering the development of the information industry.

THE SERVICE INDUSTRIES

In industry, increased business efficiency, due to office and factory automation, will shorten working hours and increase leisure time. This will give rise to a number of new demands, most of which will be met by the service sector of tertiary industry.

The tourist and sports industries will expand and provide more jobs in a number of areas. The sales of sports clothing and equipment, sports clubs, holiday clubs, the renting of boats, private aircraft and summer cottages will all profit from the increase in leisure time. With longer vacations, more disposable income, and more exposure to other

9

regions and foreign cultures through television and communication systems, people will develop the desire to travel, to visit the places they have seen on television and to learn more about other cultures.

Other entertainment fields will also benefit. The demand for theatre, movies and concerts will increase, as will the adult education industry which can offer, for example, foreign language classes for those who travel to other countries; computer, software or similar training classes to keep adults abreast of current trends; even training courses in specialised fields, including arts and crafts, to allow individuals to advance in their careers. These are just a few of the many ways in which tertiary industry will expand and the areas where jobs will be created in the future.

The impact on cultural identity

The widespread introduction of C&C systems will bring video images from all parts of the world directly into our living rooms. We will soon be able to listen to the news direct from France, Japan, the US, the Netherlands or any of a vast number of other countries. We might choose to display the current fashions in a specific city on the other side of the world on our home monitor. We will see, meet and talk to people from other nations. For example, through the video phone, friends from Germany could introduce us to the director of a famous firm, or company managers in Spain could discuss an expansion plan with the local branch in Hong Kong.

This ability to communicate and watch worldwide movements via live relay will help expand areas of common interest between nations and promote mutual understanding among humankind, dissolving the antagonism between nations, races and religious groups. The opportunity to experience the culture of another city or region of the world will lessen the instances of 'culture shock' and make it easier for people to travel. The mutual understanding which will then develop between different cultures will surely be a force for world peace.

This same ability to bring diverse cultures closer together, could also, however, lead to the dilution or gradual loss of cultural traditions in certain nations, regions and races; people would be free to choose from a variety of life-styles, dress habits and behaviour presented to them on the television screen –– some of these might seem more attractive or exotic than the traditional styles of their own regions. If we are to succeed in guarding our cultural traditions then efforts must be made at all levels of society — government, individual and business — to preserve the rich variety of cultures peculiar to each part of the world and to ensure their transmission to our descendants.

International cooperation and technology transfer

The question of international cooperation now presents itself. In order to make it possible for the whole of humankind to benefit equally from C&C systems and ensure their use in every part of the world, it will be essential for the industrialised nations to cooperate mutually in the transfer of technology and in the technological education and training of people in developing countries.

The transfer of technology will be easier once C&C systems and networks are realised. The time and space reductions these systems permit will allow companies to establish plants wherever raw materials and labour are available, regardless of the plant's distance from the home office. These plants will form the first link in a chain of technology transfer through which information and technology from the industrialised nations will be passed on to the host developing country. Moreover, through the production of goods for export, the developing countries will increase their exports and thus their trade balances.

The second link in the chain is the training and education of local personnel to work in the plants and to become specialised in information technologies. Software production, robotics programming and supervision, and telecommunications are all areas in which local employees will be trained and work. Following education and training for the local population in software production, for example, software specifically tailored to match each country's particular culture will be developed along with software for export to the industrialised countries.

In order to make technology transfer work, the industrialised countries must make a commitment to support and contribute to the development of the local telecommunications and educational infrastructures through the education and training of their personnel. Such crucial and expensive investments cannot be left as the sole burden of a single multinational or a single government. Working together, the governments of the developed and those of the developing nations can create the necessary infrastructure to support the spread of technology and its economic gains throughout the world.

The role of the Centre for Telecommunications Development

The Centre for Telecommunications Development was established following the recommendations of the Independent Commission for Worldwide Telecommunications Development. The report of that commission, known as 'The missing link', states that 'development aid for telecommunications in the developing countries should aim, first and foremost, to train manpower'. To utilise training courses to the widest extent, systems compatibility must be ensured through international cooperation.

It is hoped that the government of each country and the relevant corporations will cooperate and support the activities of the Centre for Telecommunications Development, both financially and technologically, towards the goal of enabling every person in the world to have access to a telephone by the beginning of the 21st century.

Conclusions

During the TIDE 2000 (Part 3) conference to which this paper relates, we had a teleconference between Fontainebleau, France and Tokyo, Japan. This teleconference was important as a sign of what the future holds for humankind. In a very few years, such teleconferences will be routinely conducted by government agencies, corporations, universities and research laboratories. Moreover, when C&C systems are fully installed, the whole world will become a closely knit network, with business or governmental activities conducted on a 24-hour basis. Time differences will remain, but with the aid of rapid communications and expert systems using artificial intelligence and large-volume databases, decision makers will be able to contact their counterparts directly, and make prompt and fully informed decisions.

Of course, even when it becomes technically possible to talk to any person anywhere in the world face to face via electronic media, one huge problem remains — that of language. The envisioned C&C world cannot exist without the prior development of the automated interpretation telephone/telecommunication system, which the author has proposed and believes in wholeheartedly. To make this system a reality, extensive international cooperation will be needed in order to include all the languages of the world and to agree to a common standard of information exchange. Only with this kind of participation and backing can people overcome the language barrier, really begin to communicate and fully enjoy the benefits of the future C&C networks.

ISDN, which is the first foundation in a C&C network and which we are just now in the process of introducing in an experimental version, will progress through several development stages before gaining full C&C capabilities. With the improvement in man/machine interfaces, people will come to use equipment and systems as naturally as they use their hands and feet, eventually allowing them to overcome the restrictions of time and distance. As described in this paper, C&C will come to function as the social infrastructure of the world. C&C systems will create new employment at a time of change in the economic structures of the industrialised countries, and will enrich the developing countries with new industries and opportunities. Gradually, humankind will be relieved from poverty, famine, and disease, and allowed to enjoy all the good things of life on this planet.

Koji Kobayashi

Dr Kobayashi is the present Chairman and Chief Executive Officer of NEC Corporation. He has spent his entire career, following his graduation from Tokyo Imperial University, with NEC. Aside from his many activities with the company, Dr Kobayashi is the author of Challenges to the Computer Age (Jitsugyononihonsha cte, Japan, 1968) and C&C (Computers and Communications): The Software Challenge — A Human Perspective (Simul Press Inc, Japan 1982).

The Future State of Information Technology: A Technological Assessment

Tage Frisk

The information technology industry is experiencing a pace of development without comparison in the history of industry. Over a period of just 60 years, man has seen the creation and development of the computer and its related technologies. Computing speed has increased at a factor of approximately one thousand billion times. Since the 1920s and 1930s, when science relied on mechanical mechanisms which operated at speeds of 1000 operations per second, humankind has continuously developed new and faster technologies — relays in the 1940s, tubes in the 1950s, transistors in the mid-1960s and integrated circuits in the 1970s. Today, over 10 000 000 000 operations per second can be performed by high-powered computers. By 1990, a performance level of 100 million instructions per second (mips) for general-purpose computers and 10 billion floating-point operations per second (bflops) for supercomputers will be required for many applications. The industry has, to a large extent, been technology-driven, and technological improvements will continue to have a pronounced effect on it.

The following pages highlight some of the technological aspects of recent developments and comment on the future of the industry with its implications for both managers and Europe. Major determining factors for future development include:

1 The continued price/performance improvements of basic technologies for memories, microprocessors, logic and packaging.

2 Telecommunication development with new broadband transmission media.

3 Software development, artificial intelligence and knowledge-based systems.

SIIT—C

4 Professional workstation development with emphasis on ease of use.

5 Integration of the four information media — voice, text, data and image — into one knowledge support system.

Price/performance developments in basic technologies

Price/performance improvements in scale integration of silicon chips are likely to continue to dominate microelectronic technology. The trend towards greater integration, that being the incorporation of an increased number or a broader range of functions on to the same physical structure of the chip, will increase a computer's efficiency by bringing transistors closer together on the same physical surface, thus accelerating the speed of operations and assuring higher reliability. This has led to a drop in hardware prices, a drop in the cost of complex computations and in long-distance communications.

More specifically, we can anticipate advances in the megabit chip and in greater integration in memory and logic circuits. We will soon see logic circuits with minimum dimensions below one micro, and memory chips that can store several million bits of information. Benefiting from these developments is, for example, the Personal Computer (PC). Once technically limited, PCs are now much faster with 32-bit chips versus earlier 8-bit or 16-bit chips. PC functions are increasing, leading to a broader range of potential users for the machines.

There are concurrent developments in other technologies, which for the present do not threaten the dominance of silicon technology, but will probably work as a complement to it. One of these is the Josephson technology.

Subject for the Nobel prize in physics in 1973, it had been considered a key candidate for the high-performance race. However, the progress on silicon-based technologies has been so rapid it now appears unlikely that the Josephson technology will offer enough performance advantages to offset the disadvantages of this technology, that is operation at a very low temperature.

There are yet other technologies being considered, for example gallium arsenide (GaAs) large-scale integration, which offers ultra high-speed and low-power dissipation, especially at low temperatures. This technology can also be more easily combined with silicon-based

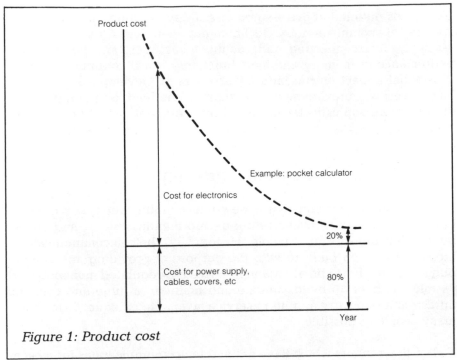

Figure 1: Product cost

technology and has natural features which make it well adapted for use in optical communication.

In fact, intelligence and computer memory is on its way to becoming a virtually free commodity. The major costs are in the box to house intelligence and memory, the units to display and print the information, the keyboard, lamps, power supplies, etc — components which are not subject to the same rate of development as basic micro-electronics. Looking at Figure 1, while the cost of electronic components in a standard electrical product have dropped as a percentage of total cost from 75 per cent to 20 per cent, the relative cost of auxiliary components has increased from 25 per cent to today's figure of 80 per cent.

The real technical challenge in microelectronics today is not in the chips themselves but in the packaging technologies for assembling, interconnecting, cooling and testing them. This can be best understood if one looks at the multilayer ceramic packaging used in IBM's large-scale processors. It is the most dense and most advanced in the industry, and IBM has successfully eliminated an entire level of packaging previously required, thereby reducing the number of interconnections by a factor of five.

The trends outlined above — greater scale integration in chips, development of complementary technologies, emphasis on packaging, assembly, interconnecting and cooling techniques, and better price/performance in memory and logic functions — will continue to have a substantial impact on the industry as a whole. Developments at these basic levels will provide new opportunities and lead to the introduction of new, more sophisticated products for industrial, scientific and consumer use.

The telecommunications industry

The creation and introduction of new telecommunications services will have a major impact on the future of information systems and on the information industry as a whole. Historically, the telecommunications industry has been built up with the purpose of providing an essential public service. It has been organised as a state-regulated monopoly and its role has been to build, operate and maintain a huge and complex infrastructure to carry a uniform service, available on equal terms, to as many people as possible.

Today, the frontiers which have defined telecommunications for most of the past century are being drastically redrawn. New requirements for technological development, changing cost structures, new patterns of consumer demand and a reshaping of the regulatory framework within which the industry operates, have forced change on this industry.

Most telecommunications organisations have not been quick to respond to a new environment. Their massive systems are based on a technology more than a century old, that of electromechanical relays and copper cables, and they are reluctant to invest in new technologies which are incompatible with the technologies used in existing networks. This is understandable given that these old networks represent an investment of over $500 billion worldwide; however, it has led to a mismatch in speed between computer systems and the communications links, which, in turn, has meant extra costs both for hardware and for programming systems. Moreover, the situation leads to inertia in the introduction of new technologies, which may continue unless the conversion from the old to the new can be achieved in such a way that a gradual introduction can be accomplished.

More technical developments are allowing the Post, Telegraph and

Telephone Authorities (PTTs) to move more quickly in this direction and will help to speed up the modernisation process. Computer technology employed in communication systems promises a signficant increase in data rates and reliability at a lower cost. With the help of digital transmission, that is pulse-code modulation links, speeds of up to six million bits per second can be obtained using a twisted pair of wires. This is approximately one thousand times more than the corresponding transmission rates over ordinary telephone lines.

Further dramatic improvements on the transmission side are possible through the use of new transmission media. The most promising of these for average distances is optical transmission of laser beam pulses via fibreglass cables. This technology would allow the transmission of a large volume of information all the way to the individual subscriber, corresponding to 50 000 telephone calls per fibreglass beam or 200 book volumes per second. Today, the world's largest copper mine is under the streets of Manhattan. But, we will mine future telecom cables on beaches where sand for fibre optics is abundant.

Putting these new technologies to work, the PTTs are now in the process of building up separate digital networks as a complement to the telephone networks. Some networks use existing transmission media, that is copper and coaxial cable, but by converting to digital transmission schemes and computer technology, these existing cables can be utilised much more effectively. In other networks, computer-controlled switches, digital transmission techniques, optical fibres etc have made their entry and will absorb most of the PTTs' investments during the 1980s, as well as becoming the most important building blocks in the public telecommunications networks. Also Private Automatic Branch Exchanges (PABXs) will become digital and, in many countries, it will become possible to connect a PABX to a central exchange via pulse code modulation links with high transmission speed. The next step is also to make the telephones digital.

A completely digital communication system will make it possible to reduce all kinds of information, speech, text, data and picture to digital flows that, combined with the services built into the network, will make it possible to offer a number of services oriented towards private or business applications. Videotext, teletext and telefax are offered, or will be offered, in several European countries.

For long distance, satellite transmission is still the best alternative offering broadband, completely digital networks without distance limitations. The earlier cost disadvantages of satellite systems are now disappearing. Less than 20 years ago there was one satellite earth station costing $50 million; now they dot the landscape and cost less than $5000.

Communications satellites are not without problems, such as the catastrophic effect if the orbital facility is lost. Transmission delays can also cause significant problems in certain applications and there is a problem of rain attenuation, particularly affecting the higher frequency transmissions. Another problem is that available space for communication satellites is limited since they all have to fly in the equator plane at the same height (22 300 miles). It might be interesting to note that American Telegraph and Telephone (AT&T) has announced its intention to take an optical transatlantic cable into operation in 1988. This will offer a high-quality transmission at lower cost than satellites.

All these developments are influenced by, and in turn influence, important changes in the economic structure of the telecommunications industry. Rapid advances in technology with shorter product life-cycles are forcing manufacturers to step up development expenditures and carriers to increase their capital investment budgets in order to remain competitive. It is becoming increasingly difficult to recover such investments through sales in just one national market.

This suggests far-reaching deregulation and liberalisation of the telecommunications market. This has already happened in the UK, where British Telecom has been stripped of its monopoly power and privatised.

Programming software

Programming will continue to be the most rapidly growing segment of the computer industry, with worldwide software revenues projected to grow twice as fast between 1982 and 1988 as overall revenues for the industry as a whole. Over the years, computer users have found that an increasing fraction of their total cost lies in programming, as they have moved from batch processing to telecommunications-oriented systems, and, finally, to distributed complex systems.

More circuits and hardware will pay for themselves, if they make the professional programmer's job more productive, but we will also need to make life easier for users who are not computer professionals — and the explosion of interest in PCs adds emphasis to this requirement.

Ideally, a user should not be conscious of 'writing' a program when asking a computer for information. One step in that direction is the relational database approach pioneered by Dr Ted Codd of IBM, in which the data appears in the form of tables and the user need only specify what is wanted, not how to get it.

Providing products that are more 'user friendly' is undoubtedly the greatest challenge facing information systems designers today. Within IBM, we have asked every unit of the company to make a major commitment to improving the ease of use, as well as the ergonomic qualities, of all our hardware and software offerings.

Professional workstations/networking to databases and remote computers

Greater interconnection between computers and workstations is being actively pursued by many participants in the information technology industry today. Development in this direction hinges upon communications technology, which is advancing rapidly, and upon networking software development, which up to this point has been complicated and costly.

However, with the increase in power of microprocessors and greater volumes of microprocessors and PCs in use, software houses can justify a wide range of application developments which rapidly increase the utility of workstations. As a result, professional workstations will become easy to program, powerful versions of PCs, networked both to similar workstations and to shared local input/output devices and files, and to large databases supported by host computers at other locations.

One example is a unique distributed computing network being developed by IBM and Carnegie-Mellon University in Pittsburgh, Pennsylvania. This involves development of software and a high-speed local area network that will give students, faculty members, researchers and professional staff access to the full Data Processing (DP) resources of the University through thousands of PC workstations. A similar project is being pursued as a joint effort between IBM and the University of Karlsruhe in Germany.

With the trend towards networking, the use of PCs and microprocessors will become more pronounced. Scale integration has given PCs the additional power needed to perform more advanced functions. Increased usage is now a direct consequence of the fact that whenever there is a need for a keyboard, a printer, a display and a box, you can add logic and memory at a very low incremental cost.

In terms of the databases to which workstations and PCs are connected, storage requirements are increasing by some 40 per cent a year. The management of massive databases to which many people need quick access requires substantial computing power, and once the majority of these databases are on-line, business growth will drive the demand for workstation access to them even higher.

Given the rapid growth in storage requirements, the large disk files will continue to play an important role. This is in spite of the fact that mechanical technology has been pushed almost to physical limits in modern disk files. However, the packaging density of the information on the magnetic media can still be significantly increased to several million bits per square centimetre, reducing further the cost per character stored.

Integration of four information media — voice, text, data and image

Developments in all four of the sectors discussed above imply a growing emphasis on the integration of information media — data, text, voice and image — into one common knowledge-support system. For example, in the office systems area, there was an emphasis on secretarial productivity; that emphasis is now shifting to total administrative productivity and, in particular, management productivity.

This means that there will be a need for products, systems and software of at least the same complexity as today's DP systems. Database, data communication requirements will be very similar to those of DP systems. Many of the databases will be common and user-interface requirements virtually identical; integration is the only practical solution.

Communications technology will begin to play a greater role in knowledge-support systems with their integration into systems which traverse the globe. Already, information and transactional systems are being actively employed by the financial community using leased, electromechanical and digital systems from the PTTs. As telecommunications technology develops, such systems may become proprietary or will, at least, be much more closely integrated into the total knowledge-support system of a company or group. Integrated Services Digital Network (ISDN) systems are, for example, making strides in this direction.

Conclusions

How will all these developments effect the information technology industry and information systems?

There are enough improvements in sight in presently known technologies, and also work-in-progress in new technologies, to guarantee a continued price/performance improvement throughout the next 10 years, or at least the same rate we have seen during the last 10 years, that is more than a 20 per cent annual improvement. The areas of greater improvement will be in semiconductor memory, microprocessors and high-performance packaging technology.

The following is a list of further conclusions:

1 Technological improvements have opened up a lot of new applications reaching all the way out to the public domain and into the home. As a result, the number of 'end users' of information systems are now counted in the millions. End-user acceptance is already the most important requirement for success of product or programme offerings and the information industry will undoubtedly become primarily end-user-driven in years to come.

2 The cost of hardware will become an insignificant inhibitor to demand by 1990. Procurement of most end-user-related products will be based on discretionary rather than investment decisions. The silicon chip will become an almost free commodity and clever packaging for serviceability and reliability will become of key importance, in particular for high-volume products.

3 The continued price/performance improvements require very high capital investments in manufacturing processes for very high-volume outputs. This increases the risks taken by manufacturers in developing and putting a given product on the market. A company could develop the wrong product or a product whose life-cycle is too short given the technological investment required.

4 There is no major breakthrough in sight for software technology. Production of software will continue to require substantial manpower efforts and programmer scarcity will remain the key bottleneck for implementation of new applications.

5 Applications development without programmers will be the key for the continued growth of the information technology industry. This means an increased emphasis on new interfaces providing the information and tools necessary for end users without programming training, to access and enter information and develop their own applications.

6 Increased integration of the information media into one powerful

knowledge-support system will lead to increased complexity. System complexity will then be one of the major inhibitors to growth in the information industry, unless ease of use is guaranteed through clever design of the end-user interface.

7 Another factor which threatens to inhibit growth in the industry is negative public opinion brought about by the unrestricted access or the misuse of information. Emphasis on the security and privacy of information must continue. Public outcries against the information industry as a whole are to be avoided.

8 In view of the enormous investment in systems hardware and application programs that has already been made around the world, ease of conversion from today's systems to systems of the future is a number one priority confronting system designers.

This is a restriction that will somewhat hamper technical progress. In some senses it is similar to the problems encountered in the telecommunications industry. However, today there are enough bright ideas about overcoming this problem to permit us to be very optimistic about the future.

SOME KEY IMPLICATIONS FOR MANAGEMENT

The extremely fast development of the information technology industry is resulting in a rapid move towards an information society. This is a challenge for management at all levels in organisations who must keep up with the fast pace of change.

The rapid introduction of new information technology products, systems and services puts a high demand on top management for making fast and wise investment decisions. Slow introduction of new technology and services can result in significant competitive disadvantages.

There is an equally big challenge for the middle manager. He must keep up with the new information tools, promote and encourage the introduction of potentially disruptive and job-displacing systems, and implement the new systems about whose technical advantages he may be ignorant or sceptical.

For these reasons, at all levels of management, well-planned, timely and ongoing education is of vital importance.

IMPLICATIONS FOR EUROPE

Europe lags behind the US and Japan in its ability to put information technology to work across the board and make technological discoveries into profitable products.

For example, Europe's part of the integrated circuits business represents only five per cent of the world market. Europe is one generation behind in memory chip technology and is entirely dependent on US licences for microprocessors. This is not due to a lack of skills and capabilities. The primary problem is national protectionism resulting in fragmented markets that are insufficient to support the high and risky investment involved. Nevertheless, Europe can catch up and is apparently dedicated to doing so. In telecommunications, which is a vital part of the information technology industry, Europe is still strong.

Actions have been taken to retain this strength through deregulation (for example British Telecom) and an EEC-initiated programme called R&D in Advanced Communication Technologies for Europe (RACE).

The European Strategic Programme for Research and Development in Information Technology (ESPRIT) programme is addressing other key areas of information technology that are relevant to Europe. These programmes have already resulted in a much closer cooperation across country borders in Europe. Some 200 projects involving 450 organisations and 1300 researchers in all EEC countries are already underway. Significant progress towards standardisation has also been achieved.

A large number of alliances between European information technology companies and US or Japanese companies will also help to compensate for the fragmented market and contribute towards a more uniform European market.

Other EEC initiatives like Basic Research in Industrial Technologies for Europe (BRITE) and Community in Education and Training for Technology (COMETT) will also pull in the same direction. While many EEC programmes are primarily precompetitive research and development efforts, the EUREKA programme, which is now supported by 19 European countries, is expected to lead to products and systems.

If well managed, the totality of the above programmes should put Europe back in a competitive position in information technology, assuming that significant progress is achieved towards the creation of a truly Common Market.

Tage Frisk

Dr Frisk is Vice President, Science and Technology, for Europe, Africa and the Middle East at IBM Europe. He has been with IBM since 1961 during which time he has been Director of Operations, European Laboratories; Line Switching Systems Director, IBM Europe, and Director of International Operations, IBM Sweden. Dr Frisk holds an MSc from Yale University and a PhD from Chalmers Institute of Technology in Gothenburg. In addition, Dr Frisk is the Director of the Arthur K Watson International Education Centre at La Hulpe, Belgium.

PART II

The Limits of Policy Making in Information Technology

To what point can the international community support the strain brought on by governments operating on their own, finding domestic, one-sided solutions to international problems posed by information technology? The spread of information technology may well lead to the creation of a 'global village'. In that global village, there may be no room to accommodate the individual political interests of a hundred or more governments.

In fact, the growth of a global village will imply the giving up of power by individual governments. Power may flow to economic interests involved in international trade, or to international organisations who may soon act as referees or policemen in the international community.

For governments, the process of relinquishing power to other parties will not be an easy one. Governments, like bureaucracies, will have the tendency to prolong their existence long after their usefulness has expired. In addition, nationalism is by no means a dead philosophy in the public eye. Political beliefs and a series of complex social philosophies accompany each government's existence.

The process of transition will, thus, be a slow one with an uncertain outcome. For now, the world must prepare itself for increasing conflict and inconsistencies in relations between nations, and between governments and industry and commerce. Methods must be devised to deal with the issues which arise and forums should be created to allow for greater global discussion of the issues. Peter Robinson discusses what present international organisations can do and proposes ways in which cooperation can be improved. Kazuo Ogura probes deeper into the issue of domestic interests versus international cooperation.

International Decisions and National Decision Makers

Kazuo Ogura

Introduction

There is today a clear and identifiable trend towards the globalisation of the economies of the world. The information technology industry plays an important role in this development. Not only have information technology products become global in character, but they serve as a vehicle for the globalisation of business in general. This double character distinguishes information technology from many other sectors. It also challenges increasingly the traditional barriers between industries within the national economies, as well as the frontiers between countries. Under these circumstances, information technology presents itself to policy makers as an immensely complex and rapidly moving area requiring new approaches to problem solving with an international perspective.

Motives for globalisation

The trend towards a more international approach can be explained by three major changes in the business environment.

First, there is an evolvement towards 'international' products. This can be understood in two senses. To begin with, an increasing number of products are being manufactured or assembled in foreign countries. However in a growing number of instances, the national affiliation of products is becoming blurred. Many goods are now, for example, designed in the US, further developed in Japan, assembled in Taiwan, packaged in France and sold in Germany with whatever brand name. In each case companies are taking advantage of national strengths to reduce their total production costs. The production savings achieved result in greater price competitiveness compared with domestically produced goods in the same product areas.

Second, along with the evolution of the individual international product comes the homogenisation of products on world markets. Cars, farm machinery, computers, clothing and cassette radios look very much the same everywhere. Many products have the same technological base and are produced using the same manufacturing processes, which, in part, explains their similarity. Over the last 10 or 15 years the degree of similarity has substantially increased.

Thirdly, developments on the product front are being amplified and magnified by the emergence of the informed consumer. This consumer is product-educated and internationally aware; he or she is accustomed to finding a wide selection of products on the market and is practised in comparing quality, price and features on an international brand basis. Consumer sophistication can be attributed to more exposure to foreign cultures through the media, to greater mobility of the consumer across borders, and to the increasing experimentation with available products at home.

What is true for the personal consumer is even more true for the industrial buyer. Rapid technological developments are forcing industrial buyers to educate themselves rapidly on new technologically advanced products, many of which come from abroad.

The globalisation of products, consumers and markets has led to increasingly intense competition in the international business environment, particularly in the sector of information technology. As a result, product life-cycles have become shorter. New products mature at an amazing rate, allowing little time for a company to earn enough on the product to cover the investment made in its creation and development. While this appears to be obvious for gadgets and games due to the intrinsically short-term interest of buyers in them, this development can also be observed for more 'serious' information technology products such as semiconductors or computers. It seems in those cases that, apart from intensive competition, the technology itself sets consistently new seeds for an evolution into a higher form, thus accelerating its own development and thereby increasingly shortening the time from innovative breakthrough to technological obsolescence.

Short product life-cycles and high R&D costs force companies to go global immediately to find a large enough market to recover the investment outlay. The stakes are becoming high for both the companies involved and for governments, who have a long-term interest in seeing their own firms prospering or at least not losing money.

The political dimension of globalisation

The pursuance of globalisation as an objective of the large multi-nationals is not a new phenomenon. However, today's globalisation differs in a number of respects. Twenty years ago, companies invested in foreign markets with the recognition that a successful foreign operation would operate independently of the home office. Close cooperation and the coordination of planning and strategy between the foreign and home office would be both impractical and undesirable: impractical due to the difficulties of communication, coordination, language and movement of personnel; undesirable because of national differences which meant that the same products or techniques that worked at home did not work abroad, and because of differences in financing and governmental practices.

Today, these differences are minimised by developments towards the homogeneous product and greater similarity of consumer demand. Financial markets and corporate finance are virtually the same everywhere and governments have taken measures which have standardised or simplified the administrative and legislative steps necessary for foreign trade or direct foreign investment.

At the same time, information technologies are opening the way for managers to change their strategic approach to foreign operations. Should they so desire, close cooperation between the home and foreign office is possible. Minute-by-minute communication and information transmission has been made possible by advances in information technologies. Foreign subsidiaries can start to take a more active part in developing strategy and in decision making. Moreover, the close connection which telecommunications advancements permit, is opening up new opportunities to exploit the advantages of the local environment and bypass the disadvantages.

The increasing activity between the various parts of a multinational firm distributed across a number of countries is conducted, in many respects, outside the control of any single government. Under these circumstances, domestic policies, whose principle objective is to guide and control economic units of a particular country, should take into account their international implications.

SIIT—D

The sector of information technology is particularly exposed to political influence due to the need to set standards for communication and computer hardware and systems. Companies are very much dependent on the extent to which their goods and services are accepted abroad. As an example, communication lines on a local basis are very marketable, but their value is six times enhanced if they are available on a national basis, and 16 times better if available on a worldwide basis.

Public R&D spending can foster the international competitiveness of national firms, thus giving them an unfair advantage. On the other hand, the exclusion of foreign firms operating within national boundaries with a domestic workforce from government-related projects, may distort competition as well.

Macro-economic effects of globalisation

With the information technology industries in the lead, business activities are being rapidly globalised and the effects of globalisation can be seen at the macro-economic level. Changes in the financial or economic fortunes of one nation rapidly impact those of its trading partners. Moreover, economic movements do not go in one direction; they can, and do, 'boomerang' back on the initiating country, leaving decision makers wary of the potential rebound effects of their policies.

The degree to which nations are interconnected and the rapidity with which events in one nation impact another became painfully clear during the October 1987 collapse in the world stock markets. Not even an entire trading day had passed before every major world financial market had followed the New York stock market in its spectacular plunge. Stock prices were not the only casualty; all other financial sectors were impacted and revised economic forecasts gave more pessimistic provisions for growth in most of the developed countries.

Evidence that there is a growth in interdependence between nations can also be found by looking at trade and financial flows. Today, these are representing ever more important amounts. Statistics on world trade flows show that these have grown faster than average growth in domestic economies.

Physical trade in goods is only part of total trade. Trade in services is growing rapidly. Bank services, tourism services, consulting services or information services are all included in this category, and have high rates of growth compared with other industries. Accurate figures on trade in services are difficult to obtain, however, its importance in the world economy is beginning to be recognised, as is evidenced by its inclusion in the forthcoming General Agreement on Tariffs and Trade (GATT) negotiations.

Beyond goods and services, there are financial trade flows. Some estimates put these as high as US$1000 trillion as compared with $2.5 trillion in world goods trade. Low estimates show financial trade flows at $100 trillion, still 40 times larger than the trade in goods. The vast majority consists of investments in foreign capital markets by large trusts, corporations or other institutional investors with internationally diversified portfolios.

Governments and globalisation

Despite the growing interdependence among nations and the increasing importance of the international implications of domestic policies, political mechanisms have not undergone substantial change and have generally not internationalised, let alone globalised. Politics is still heavily, and in most cases predominantly, anchored to the interests and concerns of domestic electorates and is rarely in tune with international considerations. This is the case particularly in those countries that began to occupy internationally recognised positions at a comparatively late stage.

This widening gap between the domestically oriented electorate, and consequently domestically oriented officials, and the stark reality of growing international interdependence could partly be filled by a dynamic political leadership in each country. But leadership is likely to encounter serious difficulties for a number of theoretical and practical reasons.

At the theoretical level, governments in most countries have been founded on the basis of sovereignty and independence. The validity of a government entirely depends upon its ability to convince its people that it holds their interests at heart and that it is pursuing policies which do not conflict with the concepts upon which it was founded. If governments are to pursue coordinated policies, it is inevitable that these policies will sometimes conflict with the principles of national sovereignty or simply not correspond with the particular objectives of the local populace.

It can be argued that it is in the nation's long-term interest to cooperate as there are other industries and other factors at stake. The willingness of a nation to capitulate on one particular issue may give it the moral force to demand a similar capitulation by a trading partner on another important issue, that is a demand for a reciprocating action.

However, there is no international tally-taker or global enforcer that can ensure that all parties are considered equal partners and receive fair treatment. If a nation gives in to international pressure on a particular issue, there is no guarantee that its sacrifices will be returned in kind. Moreover, the government in power which takes it upon itself to give in to the demands of another nation takes a political risk. The public's judgement on the issue could differ from that of the government. The public may either not have confidence in the theory of reciprocity or it may feel that the probability of reciprocity is slim.

Today, much international cooperation is justified by calling attention to the future potential for reciprocity with other nations — by claiming that sacrifices made today will be in the long-term national interest. But, as globalism grows and develops, greater and greater sacrifices will be required in order to integrate the various world economies. In the future, arguments for international cooperation based on reciprocity could appear weak and unjustified when compared to the immediate needs of a nation.

For good or for bad, governments are highly susceptible to fluctuations in public opinion. The widespread use of television for political campaigns and of computerised mailing or other systematic approaches to potential supporters, along with the trend towards more image-oriented appeal as opposed to issue-oriented campaigns, strongly influence the public's approach to politics and raise questions about the reliability of the public's judgement on more complex issues.

Beyond the theoretical debate over greater international cooperation, there are other considerations which will make greater international cooperation difficult. From a strictly practical perspective, governments are not adapted to policy formulation based on global considerations.

First, there are the politicians and policy makers who are trained and experienced in domestic politics. Most begin their careers by focusing on local issues, and work their way up the political ladder to reach national popularity. They have spent a lifetime trying to know and understand the domestic population. It is thus probably unreasonable to expect that such an individual will be as knowledgeable about foreign populations as he is about his own countrymen or that he be as adept at negotiating with foreign populations as with domestic. Even the most knowledgeable may be relatively inefficient in an international environment as compared, for example, with a chief executive officer of an international firm who has spent the better part of his life abroad.

A further criticism of political institutions relates to their internal structures. Some of these can be seen as hindering rather than fostering effective cooperation. It is argued that international affairs are often classified as sub-categories in a number of special domestically oriented ministries, while the foreign affairs ministries deal with international issues but do not have sufficient technical expertise for detailed negotiations. This problem, however, is not organisational in nature, but exemplifies the structural conflict between domestically oriented politics and internationally oriented economies.

This deep-seated problem becomes most apparent at the regional or lower levels of government. Local governments and political parties are oriented towards local problems. Politicians are elected and retain their support based on their successful handling of local interest groups. While at the national level the power of special or local interest groups somewhat diminishes, their impact on local government can be almost overpowering. Should local governments have an influence on or a say in national politics, they are likely to favour the interests of these special groups over the more general and less-represented interests of the nation as a whole.

Moreover, the structural conflict between domestic and international needs often causes delays in governments' responses to changes in industry and trade. This is critical in an industry as fast moving as the information technology sector. Huge gaps, for example, exist between the slow decision making of governments or regulatory agencies and the rapid adoption and adaptation of new technologies by enterprises. As economic and political issues become further internationalised and developments still more rapid, the more difficult it will become for governments to produce timely and well-balanced responses on a variety of problems which extend into the international arena.

Technological developments will probably widen rather than close the existing gap between the globalisation of the economies and the lagging nationalistic interests of governments. It cannot be taken for granted that the governments themselves, their politicians and constituencies will be able to take into account a considerable amount of international interests. This means that multinational firms, and business leaders in the international arena of information technology, in particular, would be required to act somewhat as 'narrowers' of conflicting interests. It would equally call for a closer cooperation between policy makers and business leaders, and increasing exchanges of views, both at national and international level.

Business, governments and international cooperation

Large international firms generally do not concern themselves very much with the political ideologies of their own governments. However, since the information technology industry is of vital interest to the military sector, the activities of the industry are of strategic importance on a national level. In the same way, large military procurement programmes document the dependency of the industry on government. Differences in approach do, however, exist. Production in the US information technology-related industry seems to be very much geared towards meeting military or strategic needs, while its counterpart in Japan is more oriented towards production for improving the quality of consumer goods.

Such differences between the US and Japan are not totally unrelated to the growing argument in the US for an increase of defence burden-sharing by Japan. It also explains to some extent the resistance of the US government to the attempted acquisition of a leading US manufacturer of semiconductors by a leading Japanese information technology firm. The conflict between national interests and the economic logic of an increasingly global industry becomes obvious.

Business is, in fact, rapidly moving towards globalisation and pushing for greater homogeneity in regulations, policies and economic systems between countries. As they expand their operations worldwide, corporations are starting to realise that their success is based not only on controllable factors within the firm, but increasingly on less controllable factors exterior to the firm, such as national infrastructures, labour receptiveness, national regulations regarding exports, imports, sales and distribution practices, and even social and cultural attitudes towards new technologies, foreign firms and work in general.

This latter point is all the more important because the application of information technologies to the production process tends to demand the wholesale introduction of new methods throughout the entire range of activities.

Companies are trying to have a greater influence on these factors and they are turning to governments to provide a framework within which they can have that influence. This has led to the politicisation of economic issues. Where this is most evident today is with regard to the telecommunications industry. Advancements in telecommunications technology can now permit the close integration of all the world's communications systems — voice, visual and data — and allow their storage and widespread distribution using computers. Up to now, the world has been populated by thousands of different communications and computer systems, only a few of which can 'talk' to one another. The associated business opportunities and the potential to bring humankind closer together has led to a phenomenal leap in interest, by major companies and industry particip-ants, in the elimination of barriers between communication systems.

Regulatory structures and systems which are country-wide, and sometimes even only region-wide, block advancement towards a world communication system. Efforts by corporations and international organis-ations to destroy these barriers are frequently thwarted, because not all firms are in favour of opening up the markets as this often implies exposure to international competition in a formerly protected area. Looking at the various pressure groups at work today, it seems that weaker firms or countries, which have already lost part of their competi-tiveness, are arguing more for keeping than for eliminating barriers.

The present dispute over the deregulation of national post and telephone/ telegraph systems involves many of these issues. The landmark decision by the US government to deregulate the communications industry puts other governments and national companies in a very uncomfortable position. They either have to react to the change or develop their own strategies and thus become pro-active. Some chose to follow the US — Japan and the UK — believing their local firms to be strong enough to withstand the new competition. But deregulation is not a policy whose success is guaranteed, at least not in the short term, as is evidenced by the problems experienced in the UK. Yet, protectionistic policies are not a solution either. Non-deregulated systems may eventually experience a loss of technological competitiveness and a relative decline in service capability.

The debate over deregulation is likely to continue for some time, with deregulated countries pushing non-deregulated countries to follow. This can be explained by the asymmetry between the international position of deregulated countries versus non-deregulated ones. If the monopoly of telecommunications is deregulated, the market is almost automatically opened up to international competition. Thus, those nations adopting deregulation policies must, out of fairness, request other nations to do likewise. In contrast, those nations sticking to the monopolised systems need not impose their own system on others. In other words, the more open the telecommunications market, the more that country has to put pressure on other countries to open their markets as well. In this context, the question of telecommunications is likely to become an important political issue among nations.

International diffusion of information technology

This, however, is not the only issue. Yet another area under discussion between nations is the ease with which information technologies are being introduced in some countries and not in others. Such differences are influencing the comparative advantages of countries. Those which have succeeded in rapidly applying and diffusing information technologies are likely to strengthen their competitiveness. In contrast, those countries slow in adopting new technologies have tended to lose their competitive edge. Using minor inventions or technologies which have a relatively limited scope of application, such countries can concentrate on different fields, leaving the more specialised technologies to other countries. Yet, information technology is so important with its economic, social and political implications, that no country can afford to abandon completely efforts to diffuse this technology within its social structure.

This latter consideration has relevance for developed countries but even more so for developing countries. This is because information technology plays an extremely important role in economic development in general, to the extent that there is concern in developing countries that existing economic gaps between North and South may widen. Bearing in mind today's R&D expenditures, it may in fact be very difficult for the developing countries to catch up, or even to avoid falling further behind in the race in information technology.

For them, however, it is the issues of the diffusion and utilisation of communication and computer systems which are of utmost importance.

There also exists a problem concerning the involvement of multinational corporations. It seems that multinational enterprises are in a position to make the best use of information technology, but their activities have increasingly fallen outside the political control of their parent governments. The concern for widening gaps and the loss of political control has made many developing countries adopt a stance which maintains that information technologies will undermine the political as well as the economic independence of the developing countries. The difficulties experienced in international dialogues on services or intellectual property rights are clearly related to the widespread political concern over the impact of new technologies on the national sovereignty of developing countries.

In sum, we are, at present, witnessing conflicts between the economic interests of industrialised countries and the political concerns of developing countries, and these conflicts appear to be intensifying as time goes on.

Globalism is advancing at a rapid pace and the more it grows and expands, the less accommodating globalised corporations and other economic interests are likely to be towards governments and their specific political needs. The diffusion of information technologies is going forward and will provide the foundation upon which many international disputes will be based. The nature and intensity of these disputes is likely to rise, causing greater instability in the international arena and fewer and fewer openings for easy compromise. International cooperation could diffuse tensions and provide the foundation for growing globalisation. Going back to the discussion of those issues which make greater international cooperation difficult, it appears that ready solutions are not available to either the practical or the theoretical issues.

A possible solution to some of the theoretical issues, which concern principally the influence of public opinion on international negotiation, could be the education of the local populace, including local politicians. Once a nation's people appreciate the importance of international issues and value them as highly as domestic issues, then the development of well-balanced, prompt and efficient policies can begin. Such a change of public opinion, however, is a very time-consuming process and involves the wholehearted participation of the press and other forms of mass media. Moreover, there will always be conflict between those pushing for a more international approach and the special interest groups who strive to have their opinions heard over and above the more general issues of international cooperation.

Some of the practical hindrances to greater international cooperation will solve themselves once the public is more attuned to global issues. Politicans will make efforts to be more internationally aware and will focus upon more cooperative methods of problem solving. Institutional rigidities, however, will continue to be a problem, as they constitute a structural rather than simply an organisational problem.

Greater consideration will also have to be given to the position of developing countries. Their national sovereignty is important to them, especially as many are smaller countries with little influence on world affairs. First, ways to diffuse information technologies in these countries must be devised. Second, the power of multinationals with regard to the developing countries should be given greater consideration by the governments of the parent countries of those corporations and by the international community as a whole. On the one hand, the multinationals can offer a great service to many nations by spreading information technologies and demonstrating their uses; on the other hand, they can serve to block the advancement of developing countries and can cause considerable political disruption.

To conclude, greater international cooperation is inevitable. It is inevitable because of greater globalisation and politicisation of business and the economies, and because of the need to guarantee the spread of information technology throughout the world so that greater economic welfare can be assured for all nations.

Kazuo Ogura

Mr Ogura is the Deputy Director General of the Economic Affairs Bureau of the Japanese Ministry of foreign affairs. His prior experience in the Japanese Diplomatic Service includes service as the Director of the North American Division of the Japanese Foreign Ministry (1977-81), as Director of the North East Asia Division (1981-84) and as a Minister at the Delegation of Japan to the Organisation for Economic Cooperation and Development in Paris (1984-87). He has a degree in law from the University of Tokyo and a degree in Economics from Cambridge University. Mr Ogura is also the author of US-Japan Trade Conflicts (1983), in English, of Twelve Faces of the United States (1982), and The Succession of Political Powers (1984), in Japanese.

International Cooperation and the Role of International Organisations

Peter Robinson

Introduction

Rapid developments in information technology are resulting in pervasive and fundamental change across the range of human activity in industry, trade, government, public services, work and leisure. One of the fall outs from the ongoing information revolution is the continuing struggle of governments to keep abreast of developments and to develop appropriate policies in a timely manner.

After providing a quick overview of some of the international organisations dealing with these issues, this paper will briefly review the development of policies related to information technology, and their effect on international organisations. Thereafter is an assessment of certain aspects of the emerging international debate which affect our ability in the international fora to agree on cooperative measures. Lastly, are the views of this author on the current requirements for improved cooperation in the international arena.

The organisations involved

The pervasive nature of information technology has meant that a growing number of international organisations are dealing with a range of international issues. The International Telecommunications Union (ITU), set up in 1865 and perhaps the longest established in the field, deals largely with technological issues — particularly coordination and planning for the interworking of domestic telecommunications networks in member countries. It provides the cooperative framework for resolving technical issues, and has been instrumental in creating the global infrastructure within which much of the increasing trade services is taking place and increasing support activities for traditional trade occur.

The ITU which consists of the International Telegraph Consultative Committee (CCITT), the International Radio Consultative Committee (CCIR), and the International Frequency Registration Board (IFRB), is also a major forum for the development of appropriate standards and protocols for the emerging Integrated Services Digital Network (ISDN), and will be involved in resolving contentious issues in its implementation. An issue such as the extent to which 'intelligence' will be built into the network, or into equipment attached to the network, will have an important impact on where major profits can be made. The ITU resolution, 'Proposals for a new regulatory framework to cater to the new situation in the field of new telecommunications services' *(ROB1)*, will be discussed at a World Administrative Telegraph and Telephone Conference (WATTC) in 1988. The results of that conference could have significant implications for trade as well as for telecommunications development.

The ITU also provides technical assistance to developing countries. A 1982 resolution *(ROB2)* expresses concern about the 'relatively low level of resources allocated to telecommunications development by international aid and investment organisations' and established a commission (the Maitland Commission) to consider recommendations for 'stimulating telecommunications development in the developing world'. The commissioners concluded that 'the role telecommunications can play, especially in economic and social development and in enhancing the quality of life, is inadequately appreciated' *(ROB3)*, and made recommendations that should help create improved telecommunications systems in developing countries.

The growing economic importance of telecommunications and the increasing frequency with which complex and sensitive telecommunications issues now arise, in the ITU discussions and elsewhere, has highlighted the fact that there is no dedicated international forum where ministers and senior officials responsible for telecommunications policies can meet to discuss and resolve the issues. The need for such a forum will escalate as issues emerge with increased frequency.

It is unlikely that the ITU will move to fill this void, although WATTC 88 will be dealing with political as well as technical issues. It has been suggested *(ROB4)* that the GATT will take over international leadership in the development of telecommunications policies. This seems unlikely, although it is clear that trade negotiations will have important implications for telecommunications policies. While telecommunications regulation has been regarded as a purely domestic matter, services regulation, as well as telecommunications regulation, has an impact on trade. In fact, the trade-distorting aspects of regulation will be a major feature of negotiations on trade in services. The activities of the General Agreement on Tariffs and Trade (GATT) over the coming months will increase pressures for an international forum to discuss and resolve the political/economic issues in telecommunications. Of particular interest in this debate will be the consideration of the role of competition, and of the issues likely to arise from international networking by major users.

The Organisation for Economic Cooperation and Development (OECD), through its Committee on Information Computer and Communications Policy (ICCP), has been active on a wide range of issues raised by developments in information technology. Today, it is attempting to fill the need for a forum for the discussion and resolution of sensitive telecommunications issues in industrialised nations. Its influence in this area is very much on the rise. Its role of consensus building has been particularly important in helping member states meet the challenges posed by the new technologies.

The European Conference of Postal and Telecommunications Administrations (CEPT) is a body consisting of the postal and telecommunications administrations from 26 countries. Up to now, it has functioned as a standards setting or technical coordination and planning body, and as such has been responsible for the adoption and application of CCITT and CCIR recommendations in the European countries. The overall objective of the group, besides standards setting, is the coordination of national policies and practices among member nations. In this respect, it is now actively involved in, for example, the ISDN project, the European Mobile Telephone System project, and the European Free-Phone Service (green number) project.

The European Community (EC), since 1984, has decided to take a more active role in the information technology sector. The R&D in Advanced Communication Technologies for Europe (RACE) and European Strategic Programme for R&D in Information Technology (ESPRIT) programmes are the result of EC initiatives. In addition, under recently adopted directives of the Council of the European Communities, the EC will be involved in creating common standards for information equipment as these relate to the 1992 push for a common market. The EC role as a determiner of guidelines in this field is likely to increase, partly due to the present need to coordinate policies between member countries in order to achieve a common market by 1992, and partly due to its capacity as a regulatory body whose directives are more or less binding on member states. Perhaps more important, the EC is not restricted to one aspect of policy making or to one sector of the industry, as are some of the other international organisations, and thus can address the full breadth of the issues involved.

The International Standards Organisation (ISO) is an independent, worldwide, non-governmental organisation with 90 standards bodies, one for each nation. It is responsible for developing and promoting standards in all sectors, with the exception of electronics and electronic engineering which are covered by a complementary organisation, the International Electrotechnical Commission (IEC). Together, the ISO and the IEC are actively involved in the development of common standards for the inter-operability of communications equipment and will continue to push for further coordination between nations in this area.

Involved in the more general issues coming from developments in the information technology sector is the World Intellectual Property Organisation (WIPO). This multilateral organisation is involved in the protection of industrial and intellectual property rights; it promotes cooperation between nations in the registration and protection of trademarks, patents and industrial design, and serves as a centralised source of information on these topics. WIPO is presently involved in the development of intellectual property protections for semiconductor chips and for literary/artistic works threatened by advancements in information technology and communications. As an international body, its main handicap is its lack of enforcement authority which makes it dependent on the voluntary cooperation of each nation for policy implementation.

The Intergovernmental Bureau for Informatics (IBI) has been active in several information technology projects in developing countries, as well as in training programmes. In 1978 it organised, jointly with the United Nations Educational, Scientific and Cultural Organisation (UNESCO), a conference on Strategies and Policies for Informatics (SPIN). It has also organised two international conferences on transborder data flow.

UNESCO has concentrated primarily on the mass-media implications of developments in information technology. The MacBride Commission *(ROB5)* dealt with problems arising from imbalances and disparities in communications among countries. Its recommendations called for a 'new world information and communication order'. UNESCO also administers the International Programme for the Development of Communication (IPDC), which deals mainly with television and broadcasting. More recently, UNESCO launched an ambitious informatics programme which may lead to an extension of its work into issues of relevance to commerce and industry.

The United Nations Conference on Trade and Development (UNCTAD) is obviously active in trade issues, with a tradition for work in services, including transborder data flows. It is likely to become an important international player in the emerging discussions on trade in services. The United Nations Centre on Transnational Corporations (UNCTC) has been the major focus of UN work on transborder data flows. It has produced some useful overview reports, as well as published country case studies and a report on remote-sensing data. Other international organisations also active in this field include The World Bank and International Telecommunications and Satellite Consortium (INTELSAT).

This quick overview cannot do justice to the work that has already been carried out, nor to the efforts now under way in these, and other, organisations to achieve greater international cooperation in dealing with the range of issues raised by developments in information technology. If this work and these efforts are to be productive, however, there are certain fundamental difficulties which must be overcome. A quick backward glance may help in achieving a greater understanding of these difficulties, and provide an insight into productive steps for the future.

From an equipment focus to an issues focus

As shown in a review of information technology policies in several different countries almost 10 years ago *(ROB6)*, there was a clear indication that, in spite of ideological differences, differences in legal systems, and different stages of policy development, there was a common thread running through policy development processes in all of the countries.

After support for research on the technology itself, the focus of policy in the early phases was on equipment. In particular, the purchase of computing equipment for government use became subject to constraints and central control, while industry support policies focused on equipment manufacture. As the use of computers increased, government procurement policies began to focus on planning for use of the equipment and on assessing the subsequent effectiveness of that use, while government support measures to industry were extended to software and the service areas.

As use became ever more pervasive through the linking of computers to the telecommunications networks, the emphasis in policy formulation switched from the equipment sector to a consideration of the impacts of the equipment's use. For example, attention in policy formulation was directed at the protection of privacy, at the implications for employment, at structural changes in industry and, more recently, at trade implications.

Finally, as the impacts of information technologies have spread throughout the economy, governments are now struggling with the coordination of potentially compatible policy approaches across the broad spectrum of economic, social, legal, cultural and political issues, where requirements often pull in opposing directions.

There has thus been a progression in policies from:
— support for technology development, through
— equipment manufacture and acquisition
— services and efficiency of use, and
— impacts of that use, to
— attempts to derive cohesive policies for a variety of issues.

By and large, institutions dealing with these issues were established in the early phases when policies focused on the equipment and on the supply side of the economic equation. While supply is still important, particularly in those countries where the availability of modern computing equipment and an adequate telecommunications infrastructure are still lacking, major international issues are now arising on the use side of the equation. This is because new information technologies have led to the growth of a 'global village', with growing interdependence among nations resulting from the increasingly pervasive use of information technology equipment. As interdependence increases, imbalances are being magnified, and domestic actions are having ripple effects in other countries; many countries, particularly smaller nations and developing countries, are experiencing growing frustration and a feeling of impotence in managing their own affairs.

Institutions still tend to deal with 'supply' and 'equipment' issues. For example, the ITU still deals with the requirements for ensuring an effective supply of telecommunications services; standards bodies still deal with standards for the supply of equipment and services; and the GATT still deals with trade in goods. The difficulty in arriving at an international agreement at the GATT to examine the requirements for trade in services stems largely from concerns about the impacts of the use of international services.

Similarly, within countries, institutions — that is government departments — still focus on the supply of new information technologies (in terms of goods or services) and have not yet developed an effective framework for focusing on the impacts and implications of information technology. Issues are usually dealt with on a piecemeal basis as they arise. The complexities of the issues, and their interrelationships, often result in conflicting policy requirements, leading to 'turf' conflicts between different government agencies. Calls for improved coordination among different government departments and agencies have arisen in a number of countries *(ROB7)*. Exacerbating the problem, battles between government departments can be transferred to the international arena in order to increase an agency's power on the domestic front.

Thus institutions, at the national and international level, have difficulty dealing with current policy requirements because they are not structured to address the more pressing issues arising from the use of new technologies. These difficulties, in turn, create problems which further hinder international cooperation.

The process of international cooperation

Difficulties in achieving international cooperation are complicated by the sensitivities associated with many of the issues in the information technology sector, and by the simplistic, confrontational debates that arise when these issues are discussed. Such debates may, unfortunately, be inevitable if sufficient attention is to be given to the issues. But, once the common awareness of an issue has developed through a confrontational approach, it is necessary to develop a common understanding through discussion and a meaningful assessment of trends and their implications. This often requires a considerable amount of time, first to dispel the misleading aspects of the simplistic approach, and, more importantly, to overcome the mistrust that builds up during the confrontational debate. It is only when a common understanding of the issue has been reached, that it is possible to move on to developing cooperative approaches for dealing with it.

This process was followed, for example, in reaching an agreement on the 1981 OECD Guidelines on the Protection of Privacy and the Transborder Flows of Personal Data *(ROB8)*, and on the 1985 Declaration on Transborder Data Flows (TBDF) *(ROB9)*. Attention was first drawn to TBDF issues by the growing concern over the risks to personal privacy generated by the increasing use of computers. It was initially felt in some areas of the private sector that privacy concerns were a cloak of respectability covering protectionist interests. From the early

SIIT—E

confrontational debate on privacy/protectionism, a common understanding of the complexity of the issues gradually developed, and an agreement was eventually reached on the guidelines.

In the following years, this author tried to draw attention to the still wider range of issues raised by TBDF. Again, a common awareness of the issues developed and a simplistic confrontational debate on 'free flow versus restrictions' then began. Discussions in the OECD Conference on TBDF in London in 1983, led to a growing common understanding. It became clear that the issues were complex, and not nearly as clear-cut as was first thought — they really had little to do with flow *per se*. It was at this point in the process that it became possible to develop the text of the declaration.

This pattern continues to apply in other areas under discussion.

Recently, there has been considerable debate in international meetings and in published material about the pros and cons of 'deregulation (or competition) versus monopoly' *(ROB10)*. Although this debate has become simplistic and confrontational, it seems to have led to a common awareness that there is an issue. Now, it is being recognised that competition and deregulation are not synonymous, and that it is not an 'either/or' situation. Monopoly and competition in telecommunications will continue to co-exist for some years to come.

The debate has progressed to more meaningful discussions, and a common understanding is beginning to develop among OECD countries. Recent changes in policy attitudes of a number of countries *(ROB11)* reflect this growing understanding. It is likely that some productive work can now begin to develop cooperative approaches for dealing with some of the real telecommunications issues reflected in the 'deregulation' debate.

In considering this one aspect of international telecommunications policy development among OECD countries, some progress has been made. Parties are in the process of passing through the simplistic/confrontational debate phase, and there are now signs that a common understanding is beginning to develop. Nevertheless, there does not appear to be an international forum that incorporates developing countries where a common understanding could be reached between developing and developed nations.

If we extend our analysis to consider other issues raised by use of the new information technologies, such as trade in services, there is again a clear lack of an awareness- and understanding-building forum that includes developing countries. The OECD, with its relatively new committee for Information, Computer and Communications Policy (ICCP) *(ROB12)*, has provided, for the industrialised countries, an overview of the range of issues raised by information technology. It has also provided an opportunity to develop some cohesion in attitudes towards the issues and to achieve international cooperation in dealing with them. However, as long as the developing countries are excluded from a consensus-building process of this sort, broad international cooperation is unlikely to be achieved *(ROB13)*.

Whether this requirement can be met by another international organisation, or by changes in an existing organisation, will require further consideration. It is questionable whether any government will agree to fund a new organisation, yet the potential benefits could, with sufficient goodwill, far outweigh the costs. The major risk in creating a new organisation is the creation of a forum for political posturing, as many of the issues are still very sensitive.

In reviewing the various needs in the area of information technology, consideration should be given to the relative advantages and disadvantages of regional versus global (for example UN) organisations, and how the two types can complement each other. One of the main advantages of a regional organisation (such as the EEC), is that it tends to contain like-minded countries, so that understanding and agreement can be more easily achieved. The main disadvantage is that the more work is concentrated in regional organisations, the more fragmented is the understanding and agreement, and the greater is the risk of entrenched divergent attitudes.

The extreme of a 'regional agreement' is a 'bilateral agreement'. Concerns have been raised about a growing tendency to bilateralism, and the potential for a complex patchwork of international rules and regulations. On the other hand, it can be argued that international agreement on the issues raised by developments in information technology is essential and becoming more urgent, and that an agreement at the bilateral level can act either as a model or a catalyst for wider multilateral agreement.

Particularly important at this time is the need for a forum (to include the developing countries) for consensus-building in regard to the telecommunications and data aspects. Such a forum is urgently needed, not only because of the rapid pace of change in this area and the sensitivities surrounding the issues, but because these services are central to increasing trade in other services (banking, for example), and are providing growing support to traditional trade in goods *(ROB14)*. If the GATT is to serve as this forum in the midst of negotiations on trade, it will need to ensure sufficient isolation and buffering from the confrontational negotiations environment.

Alternative approaches to international cooperation

So far, this discussion has concentrated primarily on the awareness- and understanding-building role of international organisations — where there is currently a major requirement — and on their role in developing cooperative approaches for dealing with issues, and in providing guidance on possible government actions. A further role that might be considered is that of monitoring the effects of cooperation and joint action. In the OECD, for example, there have been reviews of national science and technology policy. Because of the crucial importance of information technology in the modern world, similar reviews of information technology-related policies may now be beneficial.

In addition to the direct work of international governmental organisations, three other approaches need to be considered, both in terms of complementing the work of those organisations, and in filling some of the gaps that governmental organisations cannot cover.

First, for example, consideration should be given to the role of universities. International understanding could be improved through cooperative research among universities in different countries on specific aspects of the information technology issues. For example, it may be possible to initiate a research project on the potential impact of selected types and levels of competition (mixed with monopoly) in the provision of telecommunications and other data-related services. Researchers in different countries, approaching it from different perspectives, could develop useful comparative results. Different cultural attitudes towards information, and towards consensus or confrontation, might also have an important bearing on the research. From a Canadian perspective, for example, the benefits of cooperative research between Canadian experts and experts from Japan, Australia, China, South Korea and other Pacific countries could be substantial. For, while the Atlantic will continue to be important in terms of international data services, it is the Pacific that will become a new major focus of dynamic change. Cooperative research of this kind would also help to develop more informed debate both domestically and internationally.

In general, international organisations have not attempted to raise public consciousness, but have tended to direct their work towards selected audiences. Concern has been expressed (at the TIDE 2000 Conference in Tokyo, for example) about a lack of public, as well as government, awareness of trends and issues, and a possible need for attention to be directed towards this problem by international organisations.

A second approach, complementing the work of international organis-ations, is to encourage the private sector to increase its international role by helping industry participants and customers to deal with emerging information technology issues *(ROB15)*. It is interesting to note, for example, that the voice of users of information technology — in the International Chamber of Commerce (ICC) and in the International Telecommunications Users Group (INTUG) — is becoming louder. Still, the international business community could do more to develop the common awareness and common understanding so essential to inter-national policy cooperation, through, for example, providing funds for the sort of cooperative research outlined above. The private sector can also help in raising public consciousness of the issues and in promoting more informed debate.

A different approach is demonstrated by the Atwater Institute in Mon-treal. This organisation has been formed at the initiative of the Canadian private sector, and has taken on the task of increasing awareness and developing understanding of information technology issues. It has not sought government funding, but is now trying to obtain funds from industry in other countries. Its conference last year brought together academics, and government and industry representatives from a number of industrialised and developing countries *(ROB16)*. This is a new organisation with good potential to become a major player in promoting international cooperation on information technology issues.

A third approach to complement the work of the international organis-ations would be the creation of a 'wise persons group'. It would meet periodically (once or, at most, twice a year) to review trends and issues, the way in which they were being handled, and to suggest priority items for attention in international organisations, in unversity research, or in the private sector.

Conclusion

As interdependence among nations increases, and as current imbalances are magnified, there will be a need to address problems associated with those imbalances in a meaningful way. Some of the current difficulties in doing this have been addressed in this paper and, in addition, suggestions have been made which could aid in redressing these imbalances. If nothing is done, the OECD will continue to assist the industrialised countries in developing common awareness, common understanding and a cooperative approach for dealing with information technology issues. International business associations will continue to perform similar functions for private sector interests. It is therefore clear that, if developing countries are to deal effectively with industrialised countries and industry, they too must become a part of such a process. This will not only help the developing countries themselves, but will also be in the interest of the industrialised nations and industry, if broad international cooperation is to be achieved. Without greater international cooperation and the complementary work that can be carried out by universities, by the private sector and by a 'wise persons group', there is a very difficult road ahead with parties caught in confrontational debates, with escalating sensitivities and burgeoning frustrations.

References

ROB1
International Telecommunications Convention Nairobi
Resolution no 10 pp 238-239
(1982)

ROB2
See ROB5
Resolution no 20
pp 254-256
Also reproduced as Appendix 1 pp 71-72 in *ROB3* below

ROB3
'The missing link'
Rep of the Independent Commission for Worldwide Telecommunications Development (the Maitland Commission)
p 4
The Intl Telecommunications Union, Geneva
(Dec 1984)

ROB4
Cowhey P
'International trade and telecommunications'
Paper presented at the Conf on Telecommunications and Business, Urban

Regional, National and Intl Development Ottawa
Sponsored by the Canadian Institute for Research on Regional Development, and the Canadian Department of Communications
(Nov 1986)

ROB5
'Many voices, one world'
Rep by the Intl Commission for the Study of Communications Problems (the MacBride Commission) UNESCO Paris
The recommendations on pp 269-270 deal with the call for a 'new world information and communications order'
(1980)

ROB6
Robinson P and Shackelton L A
'National policies and the development of automatic data processing'
Prepared for Data and Development Marseille
(1979)

ROB7
Robinson P
'Effective coordination for information technology policies'
Prepared for the OECD-sponsored seminar on The Role of Government, the Private Sector and the Professional IT Community Istanbul
(Nov 1986)

ROB8
'Guidelines on the protection of privacy and the transborder flows of personal data'
OECD Paris (1981)

ROB9
'Declaration on transborder data flows'
PRESS/A(85)30, OECD Paris
(1981)

ROB10
'Monopoly and competition in the provision of telecommunications services: a survey of the issues'
Rep prepared by the OECD Secretariat for the Special Session of the Committee on Information, Computer and Communications Policy on Intl Implications of Changing Market Structures in Telecommunications Services
(Nov 1982)

ROB11
Wieland B
'Current trends in telecommunications policy'
Intermedia
vol 14 no 6
(Nov 1986)

ROB12
'Information, computer and communications policies for the 80s'
At the 1980 High Level Conf
The French Minister of Industry proposed the creation of a committee to deal with the growing range of important information technology issues. In Apr 1982, the Committee for Information Computer and Communications Policy (ICCP) was established, by elevating the earlier Working Party to committee status

ROB13
Robinson P
'The outlook for a multilateral agreement on transborder data services'
Paper presented at the Conf on Canadian-American Telecommunications in the Global Context
Univ of Vermont
(Oct 1986)

See also

Robinson P
'An intl policy framework for data and data services: the current debate in intl organisations'
Paper presented at the Conf on Towards an Intl Service and Information Economy: A New Challenge for the Third World
New York
Sponsored by the Friedrich Ebert Foundation
(Feb 1987)

ROB14
Robinson P
'Telecommunications trade and transborder data flows'
Telecommunications Policy
(Dec 1985)

ROB15
Sauvant K P
'Intl transactions in services: the politics of transborder data flows'
no 1 p 194

Atwater Series on the Information Economy Boulder
Westview Press
(1986)

ROB16
Rep on First Atwater Conf in TDR (Transnational Data Rep)
vol IX no 12
(Dec 1986)

Peter Robinson

Dr Robinson presently holds the position of Special Advisor on International Informatics in the Canadian Department of Communications. Recently he served as Chairman of the OECD Working Party on Transborder Data Flows and participated in advisory meetings at the UN Centre on Transnational Corporations. During his career, Dr Robinson has been a Director of the Statistical Research Service of the Canadian Department of Agriculture, and the Director of Programmes for the Canadian Computer/Communications Task Force.

PART III

International Competition and Collaboration in Information Technology

The nature of economic competition is changing. Corporations and nations are simultaneously becoming more competitive and more cooperative, hoping that together these two approaches will lead to greater gains for all. Maybe, man is not putting into practice what has long been known to philosophers and game theorists — that the only game better than a zero-sum game is a win-win game where both players are winners.

Economies of scale and scope together with towering R&D costs and shorter life-cycles, make greater internationalisation a pre-condition for success in an increasingly global marketplace. For both competing firms and countries, their future welfare and survival is at stake.

At the same time, these parties are cooperating. They are working towards better coordination, greater standardisation and some homogenisation of systems and products. Companies are forming joint ventures and countries are sponsoring joint research projects.

Where will all this activity in the international community lead; is greater interdependence inevitable; what does this imply for decision makers? Many of these issues are addressed by the following three authors. Louis Turner presents the situation in a competitive format, comparing the relative position of Japan against the other two contenders for world economic strength, the US and Europe. Warren Davis describes to what degree competition has intensified, yet, points out that cooperation represents a cross current to that competition. Strategic alliances, the present popular form of cooperation between corporations, are explored by Adrian Norman.

International Competitiveness: Implications for Europe, the US and Japan

Louis Turner

The comparative analysis of underlying international competitiveness is never easy, but it is particularly difficult at the moment. This is because we are only just starting to grapple with the question of Japan's true long-term innovative strengths and weaknesses.

Up to now, it has been easy to assume that we can extrapolate from Japan's past success in catching up with her industrialised competitors into a future where she moves inexorably ahead of them. It is this uncritical belief in Japan's industrial invincibility which explains some of the bitterness in her trade relations with older established economies.

On the other hand, some observers of the Japanese scene are less convinced that Japan's past success is a sound guide to the future. They point to the country's continuing deficit on the technological balance of payments. They raise questions about whether the Japanese educational system stresses conformity over the individualism needed to innovate. They wonder whether Japan will be as successful as in the past when she moves away from relatively standardised products like video recorders and cars, to more complex industries systems such as aircraft, and to more 'software'-constrained products such as computers or financial services.

There are, of course, counters to these arguments. Japan now leads the world in the registration of domestic patents, and its deficit on the technological balance of payments is shrinking. If the country's educational system has its faults, its achievements in numeracy and literacy look increasingly convincing as serious international comparisons are carried out; only in the US does as large a proportion of its students stay on to higher education (see Table 1).

The number of research scientists and engineers per 1000 of the workforce is the second highest in the Organisation for Economic

Table 1: Proportion of a generation entering higher education

Country	Entrants for further education as a percentage of generation (c 1980)
Japan	62
United States	62
Sweden	25
Germany	20
Denmark	33
France	34
Italy	25
Finland	10
Netherlands	26
United Kingdom	29

Source: OECD

Cooperation and Development (OECD) world (see Table 2). On the industrial front, it can be argued that selective government-industry research programmes can be used to overcome weaknesses in sectors where Japan is currently weak.

Table 2: Number of research scientists and engineers per 1000 of labour force, 1981

US	6.2
Japan	5.4
Germany	4.7
UK	3.9
Norway	3.8
France	3.6

Source: OECD

The debate on such issues is bound to remain inconclusive for a while, until the effects of the chronically undervalued yen are countered by its recent strengthening. However, some general points are relatively non-controversial. First, Japan's share of world high-technology exports has risen steadily over recent decades, until she is now outranked only by the US. Second, although Japan's per capita R&D expenditure remains quite modest , it is not distorted by a heavy bias toward the defence sector, which a number of critics believe explains some of the apparently low commercial productivity of research in countries like the US and the UK. (Military research accounts for 0.35 per cent of Japan's total R&D effort, compared with 22 per cent in France, 27 per cent in the UK and 28 per cent in the US). Third, few people now underestimate the basic competence of Japanese management, which has fully proved itself in recent decades. Although Japanese companies are not particularly experienced overseas investors, the dynamism of their domestic and export markets has let them become the largest cadre of giant companies after those of the US.

Discussions of the perceived Japanese industrial strengths tend to assume that Japan is now competing directly with the US for the position of the world's most technologically dynamic economy. Western Europe tends now to be dismissed as an 'also ran'. This shows up in indicators such as that its companies only have a (falling) 10 per cent of the world market for microchips. A recent Fortune survey of where the US, Japan, Western Europe and the USSR stand in key industries like computers, life sciences, advanced materials and opto-electronics had Europe firmly in third place across the board. Defenders of Europe will point to sectors such as aerospace and chemicals where Europe's performance is considerably stronger, though, even here, the Europeans remain behind the US.

This paper is designed to throw light on these preconceptions of a declining US dominance, Japanese dynamism and European sclerosis by looking at the evidence from within the information and communication technology sectors.

Comparative competitiveness by sector

'Information and communication technology' covers a lot of different activities. At the micro level, there is the cut-throat world of semiconductors, which has its own subdivisions of memories, microprocessors, logic chips etc. One then ranges through computers into telecommunications, which not only involve ground hardware but satellite capabilities. However, one has to deal not just with the electronic hardware, but with the traffic which these technologies support. This means that we need to account for enhanced services such as Local Area Networks (LANs), financial databases etc.

Accepting that generalisations across such a range of technologies and activities are bound to be dangerous, a starting point for debate could be the following propositions:

1 That Japan is featuring strongly in most sectors where sheer manufacturing and technical expertise are crucial.

2 That the US has defensible strengths in software-intensive sectors (and that the trend in most of these sectors is towards greater software intensity).

3 That Europe has been losing ground almost across the board against both Japan and the US.

SEMICONDUCTORS

This is the sector (see Table 3) *par excellence*, where the relative gains by the Japanese are clearest, with symbolically, NEC overtaking Texas Instruments in 1985 to become the world's largest chip-maker (with Hitachi and Toshiba following into second and third position in 1986). Japan's share of worldwide integrated circuit sales is currently around 38 per cent, up from some 30 per cent in 1982. In the latest generation of commodity memory chips (256k Dynamic Random Access Memory (DRAMs)), Japanese companies have taken around 85 per cent. Although this still leaves the US industry with around 50 per cent of the total semiconductor market, such Japanese incursions have proved unsettling to the established American industry.

Table 3: Semiconductor producers: dependence on semiconductors

Japanese firms	Semiconductor sales as a percentage of total sales	US firms	Percentage
NEC	17.8	AMD	89
Fujitsu	6.7	Fairchild	69
Toshiba	5.5	Intel	75
Hitachi	4.1	Mostek	93
Mitsubishi	3.8	Motorola	31
Matsushita	2.3	National	85
		Texas Instruments	36

Source: New Scientist 1 May 1986

There are a number of explanations for this Japanese success which tell us something about the underlying competitive strengths of Japan. First, its government clearly did have a catalytic role to play through the Ministry of International Trade and Industry's (MITI) Very Large-Scale Integration (VLSI) programme which was run between 1976 and 1979, and involved the Nippon Telegraph and Telephone Corporation (NTT), along with five of the country's leading electronics companies. The latter had their attention focused on the need to diversify out of consumer-oriented integrated circuits, into those needed for high growth sectors such as computers and telecommunications. Emphasis was also paid to the upgrading of process technology (see Table 4). Subsequent MITI-led programmes have concentrated on opto-electronics, supercomputing and new function elements. Whatever the impact of these latter programmes, it is generally accepted that the VLSI programme was extremely important in the arrival of Japanese chip manufacturers on the world stage (see Table 5).

Table 4: Comparison of Japan versus US in integrated circuit technical strength

		Japan	US
1	Product planning		•
2	System and circuit technology		•
3	Computer-aided design technology	•	•
4	Device technology		•
5	Assembling and testing technology	•	
6	Quality control	•	
7	Mask technology	•	
8	Integrated circuit manufacturing equipment		•
9	Materials		•
10	Cleanroom and pollution prevention technology	•	

Note: • denotes relative superiority

Source: Journal of the Communication Engineers of Japan June 1980
Communication Engineers of Japan

A second factor which is widely claimed to explain the rise of the Japanese industry is the extent to which the Japanese companies leading the onslaught have been vertically integrated, combining chip manufacture with end-use applications. This is widely seen to contrast with the over-specialisation of American chip manufacturers like AMD, Fairchild, Intel, Mostek, National and so on. As the scale of investment needed for each generation of chips has escalated (a figure of over $100 million per chip generation is now mentioned), the specialised American chip producers have just not had the financial muscle to stay fully competitive. There has thus been a movement to bring some of these specialist producers within a more integrated framework (IBM's temporary minority stake in Intel was a harbinger as, more arguably, is the tie-up between AMD and Sony).

Japan's strengths are, however, not uniform throughout the semiconductor sector. There is still a clear correlation between Japanese successes and the extent to which a specific product can be standardised. The more design intensive a chip is, the weaker the Japanese position seems to be. So, while Japanese companies' shares of the world memory chip market rose from 30 per cent in 1981 to 53 per cent in 1985, US companies produced 56 per cent of the world's microcprocessors, and the same proportion of logic circuits. (Europe supplied 13 per cent of the logic market, seven per cent of memories and six per cent of microprocessors.)

SIIT—F

Table 5: Government R&D assistance

	Date	Project	US $ million	Comments
Australia	1983-84	CSIRO Research (1)	0.6	
Canada	1981	Gallium arsenide devices	1.7	
US	1978-84	VHSIC Phase 1 and	341.4	
	1978-82	non-VHSIC R&D (2)	200.5	
	1985-89	VHSIC Phase 2	340.3	
Japan	1975-81	LSI ICs for computer, telecommunications and microwave (3)	180.0	
	1976-79	VLSI (4)	121.2	Repayment
	1980-91	Opto-electronics	77.5	required
	1982-90	Supercomputer	92.3	Consignment
	1982-89	New Function elements	100.4	payment (no refunding)
EC	1983-84	ESPRIT Pilot Project (5)	11.4	
	1982-85	Microelectronics Programme	32.0	EC share
	1984-89	ESPRIT	744.0	EC share
France	1982-86	2nd Components Plan	487.0	
Germany	1974-78	BMFT Electronic Components (6)	157.0	R&D assistance
	1981-82	BMFT Electronic Components	110.0	to industry and
	1981-84	VDI R&D (7)	0.9	institutions
	1984-88	Submicron Technology	169.0	
UK	1983-88	Advanced Information Technology Programme	308.5	
Finland	1982-85	CMOS Progress Technology (8)	7.0	Funds for equipment and salaries
Sweden	1980-85	National Board for Technical Development	47.3	Grants to technical schools

Source: OECD Observer

The Japanese have effectively come to dominate the largest segment of the semiconductor market, but one can still debate whether this means they will be able automatically to sweep into the more complex, but economically less important markets which the US companies are still defending.

There are, in fact, signs that the American and, to a much lesser extent, European industries are trying to take advantage of their greater experience in design intensive sectors. In particular, they are negotiating much more toughly on licensing matters, and are trying to move away from the readily acceptable cross-licensing agreements they had traditionally signed with their Japanese competitors. There has been the recent Californian court case in which Intel has been arguing (against NEC) that the microcodes at the heart of its microprocessors are open to protection under US copyright law.

Only time will tell how significant the eventual decision, in this case, will prove to be. What it does signify is the belief in the US camp that one reason for Japan's success is that the latter's companies were able to copy American designs and then manufacture the chips more cheaply. Obviously, this is a contentious argument, and Japanese companies argue that they are developing their own designs which American companies now need to absorb in their own turn.

For the moment, there are few signs that West Europe's long decline throughout most of this sector is going to be reversed. Explanations for Europe's weakness normally touch on the industry's fragmentation between different nations, or the absence of a dominant end user, such as America's defence establishment or Japan's consumer electronics sector. Any explanation probably also needs to take into account the specific strategies followed by European companies, which have emphasised the development of customised rather than commodity chips. Since the relative importance of custom chips such as gate arrays is growing, European companies should have a defensible niche. However, it looks as though they have, even here, been losing market share quite rapidly. Between 1980 and 1985, Europe's share of gate arrays fell from 30 per cent to 10 per cent.

SOFTWARE

Despite Europe's weakness across semiconductors, there are signs of Japanese vulnerability, most specifically in the area of software. Some of the reasons for this weakness are uncontroversial. In particular, the complexities of the Japanese language held back typewriters, with the result that the Japanese have simply not acquired the keyboard culture which, in the US and Europe, has facilitated the acceptance of personal computers which, in turn, has produced the cadres of people who have turned naturally to computer software development.

In Japan, software development has been a low prestige occupation, concentrating on producing bespoke applications for computer purchasers, rather than on the development of the kind of mass-market packages which are found elsewhere in the world (Lotus 1-2-3, Wordstar etc). Whatever the full implications for Japan's competitive position in other parts of the information technology industry, I merely note here that the Japanese software scene is very different from those in the US and Western Europe. In fact, some of the reasons for their weakness in the software field have resulted in compensating strengths elsewhere in the general information technology area. Thus, the complexity of Japanese characters has forced the development of their printer industry. Again, the fear of keyboards has meant an emphasis on facsimile transmission, in which Japan has a world lead. Finally, the problems concerning the isolation of Japanese speakers and readers (which, among other things, make it difficult for Western software to find ready markets in Japan), mean that there is a particularly urgent dimension to Japan's search for improved machine translation which, if successful, will serve them well in at least one part of tomorrow's markets.

The Japanese response to their weakness in software has been to launch a new MITI project known as Sigma. The aim is to automate the production of software, and to eliminate much of the duplication which arises in a relatively troubled industry. Whether this particular MITI initiative will have the catalytic impact that the VLSI one had for general chip production still remains to be seen. Much of what one concludes about Japan's potential in the more complex information and communication systems will rest on whether one believes that Japan can conquer its software problems.

COMPUTERS

Once one moves away from chips to the design and marketing of computer systems (see Table 6), the balance of advantage swings more towards the US. Certainly, Japan has been gaining, but her future looks more problematical. The Europeans, once again, seem to be being relegated to third position.

For the moment, IBM remains the dominant force in the world industry, even though it has recently been having a more troubled existence than it has been used to. The lesson from this colossus is that sheer technical excellence is not everything. Good products have to be marketed and within the computing field this means developing them around a marketable operating system, encouraging the development of a substantial software base, the provision of support staff etc. Without downplaying IBM's technical expertise, much of its success in the Personal Computer (PC) sector has come from sheer marketing power.

There is, of course, competition to IBM and its smaller US competitors both in Japan and Western Europe. Many observers have tended to be

Table 6: Top computer companies — 1985

	Computer-related revenue $billion	As percentage of total revenue
IBM	48.6	97.0
Unisys	9.6	89.4
DEC	7.0	100.0
Fujitsu	4.3	65.7
NCR	3.9	90.0
NEC	3.8	38.0
Control Data	3.7	100.0
Hewlett-Packard	3.7	56.0
Siemens	3.3	17.6
Hitachi	2.9	13.8
Olivetti	2.5	82.0
Wang Laboratories	2.4	100.0

Source: Datamation

somewhat more impressed with the Japanese potential than with the European one. However, few would suggest that the Japanese computer companies are about to do to IBM what they have managed to do to the semiconductor competition.

Certainly, within Japan, IBM has been kept to an unusual (for it) second place, but the Japanese companies have not counted for much so far outside Japan itself. Where they have been able to sell components and peripherals, these companies have done well, providing about 30 per cent of the wholesale value of the American PC market. However, Japanese PCs have taken less than two per cent of this market, indicating that overall control of the design and marketing of PCs is still vested in IBM, the Compaqs and the Apples, and an ever-widening array of providers of clones.

Japan's relative failure to penetrate the PC market is instructive, because it runs counter to so much success it has had in earlier, apparently quite similar markets like consumer electronics. What seems to have happened is that the Japanese industry was slow in coming to terms with the IBM PC-DOS standard for PCs, and failed to establish any competing standard outside Japan itself. In home computers, where Japan did try to create an international standard, MSX, its failure to impose this on a fragmented world market was very noticeable.

The Europeans have been no more successful than the Japanese in entering world markets, but they started from a much weaker position in their home markets in Western Europe, itself. Firms like Olivetti, Norsk

Data and Nixdorf have found niches, but are nowhere near strong enough to guarantee themselves long-term independence.

The interesting questions are about the future. IBM has clearly made some defensive moves: its R&D expenditure remains massive; it is investing heavily in automation to keep costs down; it is building enhanceability into its product design by raising the importance of microcodes in its products' operating systems. All of this will make life more difficult for the competition — particularly in Japan, whose software weakness has already been commented upon.

The interesting question is whether Japanese companies can leapfrog IBM and the Western competition by developing radical new approaches to coming generations of computers. The programme which is designed to achieve this is the Fifth Generation programme which is trying to produce just such a set of breakthroughs in artificial intelligence and parallel processing.

The reports which are coming through about this programme are somewhat inconclusive, but it would be surprising if it has the impact of the earlier VLSI programme. For one thing, its very creation has triggered off a number of competing programmes around the world, from European Strategic Programme for R&D in Information Technology (ESPRIT) and national programmes like Alvey in West Europe, to American ventures such as Microelectronics and Computer Technology Corporation (MCC) and the work of the Defence Advanced Research Projects Agency (DARPA) in the area of supercomputers. For another thing, all this Fifth Generation work is having to identify paths into the future, which is a very different kind of operation from the catch up and improvement operation which the MITI programmes of the 1970s still were. It is perfectly possible that the Japanese emphasis on logical inference will indeed be the way forward, but that is by no means guaranteed.

TELECOMMUNICATIONS

The telecommunications world (see Table 7) has entered a period of major upheaval. Not only are traditional telecommunications utilities having to come to terms with the convergence of computing and telecommunications, but a number of national authorities have been liberalising this sector, thus adding a further element of competition to a traditionally protected industry. With its break up of the AT&T monopoly, the US has pushed furthest ahead with such liberalisation, with the UK and Japan leading the second wave of liberalisers. Most of the rest of Europe is proving reluctant to move away from heavy regulation of this sector.

This tradition of national regulation and protection has meant that intercontinental competition has so far been muted, so that trade figures tell us little about long-term comparative strengths and weaknesses round the world. The underlying scale economies (the next range of public digital switches will cost at least $1 billion to develop) are rapidly forcing the core telecommunications companies to develop global strategies, often in conjunction with other international players, in order to keep abreast of all the developments which are currently being called for.

Table 7: World suppliers of digital public exchange equipment ranked by 'turnover' (figures for 1985 or nearest comparable period)

		£m	Percentage of total
1	Alcatel	1550	19.5
2	AT&T	1350	16.9
3	Northern Telecom	1000	12.6
4	NEC/Fujitsu/Hitachi	1000	12.6
5	Siemens	950	12.0
6	LM Ericsson	750	9.4
7	GTE	350	4.2
8	Plessey (inc £70m Stromberg Carllson)	330	4.1
9	GEC	260	3.3
10	Italtel	180	2.3
11	Philips (AT&T Equipment)	130	1.6
	Others	120	1.5
		7970	100.0
	Alcatel CIT	700	8.8
	Ex-ITT *	850	10.7

* These two merged in January 1987 to form Alcatel

Source: Monopolies and Mergers Commission

This is one of the handful of industrial sectors (other than office automation and ordnance) where US companies have actually been gaining market share, and there are few signs that this strength will be sapped. Both from within the telecommunications tradition (AT&T) and from without (IBM), the US possesses companies with the financial strength, technological tradition and global vision which should see them holding off the competition. In addition, the fact that the US has deregulated this sector should stoke the technological and marketing ferment which will keep good companies at the forefront of the world industry.

The Western Europeans have been relatively strong in this sector, with companies such as Siemens, Ericsson, Alcatel-Thomson, Philips, GEC,

Plessey and ItalTel all in the top rankings. Europe has a positive trade balance of some $1.4 billion (1985), even though it is in deficit with both the US and Japan. However, market share is slipping. The US has 33 per cent, the EC has 31 per cent (down from 35 per cent in 1983), with Japan at 17 per cent (up from 12 per cent). This erosion of a strong position convinces many observers that the European industry has some long-term problems.

On this analysis, the blame is attributed to a number of factors. First, the fragmentation of Europe into a series of national markets is beginning to matter. When a manufacturer may well need between six to eight per cent of the world market to justify developing a new switching technology, a fragmented Europe cannot yet provide a market of sufficient size. On top of that, the duplication of effort encouraged by relatively protected national markets takes its toll in several ways. For instance, the European industry uses six times more software resources than the American one does. A new firm trying to enter Europe's modem or Private Automatic Branch Exchange (PABX) market will be faced with regulatory costs roughly 100 times greater than those incurred in the US.

The ultimate cause for pessimism within Europe comes from the relative lack of demand for telecommunications products. In 1985, telecommunications usage was $32 per head in Europe, in comparison with $46 in Japan and $80 in the US. The reasons for this weakness in demand can be debated, but the chances are high that it is related quite strongly to the over-regulation of the industry in most of the continent, with West Germany's Bundespost being a classic example of how a heavily paternalistic regulatory authority can stifle innovation and competition within the telecommunications industry of one of the richest economies in Europe. Obviously, there are other factors at work, for Japan's liberalisation has come too recently to explain the higher consumption figures in that country. However, the failure of Europe to develop a true common market in telecommunications has to be behind much of the weakness we are starting to see in Europe's performance.

As the statistics show, Japan starts from a relatively weak position in world telecommunications markets, though she has been gaining ground. On the regulatory front, she now has in place a system of internal competition which, though not as extensive as that found in the US, is probably more than that seen in Britain and certainly is well ahead of that seen elsewhere in Western Europe. For the moment, the competition with Japan is primarily between Japanese equipment suppliers, though, under considerable foreign pressure, foreigners like Northern Telecom, IBM and Hughes Telecommunications have been picking up some orders.

There are probably two main tests ahead for the Japanese industry. First, in an industry where global alliances to reap scale advantages seem to matter a great deal, one senses that firms like IBM, AT&T, Alcatel, Olivetti, Philips *et al* are forming networks of international alliances which may well lock Japanese ones into second-best solutions as they try later to follow the same route. Secondly, if one accepts that Japan does have problems in software, then it will be interesting to see if her companies can come to terms with an industry where software/hardware relationships are being overturned. On some estimates, by 1990, about 80 per cent of the end cost of telecommunications equipment will be for software development. Can the Japanese companies master this challenge?

One other area worth debating is how demanding end markets are for telecommunications products in the different parts of the Triad. Here, the author has no figures, merely some impressions.

Obviously, the demands of the corporate sector on the telecommunications industry are one of the prime forces for change on the industry. The constant need to link larger numbers of computers to each other; the desire to transmit pictures, sound and data over the same system; the need to be instantaneously in touch with (particularly, financial) developments throughout the world, all push the telecommunications industry into supplying new products.

On balance, it looks as though the US is taking the lead in the development of many of the resultant new products and services, though one may be discounting Japanese developments because of the language barrier. Certainly, in the field of electronic databases, once one has discounted the British company Reuters, American information providers tend to dominate. One thinks of Dow Jones and its Telerate subsidiary, AT&T's links with Quotron, Reader's Digest's The Source, Compuserve *et al*. These are all services which have developed commercially.

With the notable exception of Reuters, the Europeans seem well behind the Americans in the whole area of commercial databases. Where Europe has taken a lead, as in videotex Post, Telegraph and Telephone authorities (PTTs) have tended to take the initiative. In general, though, it is the linguistic fragmentation of Europe which counts against it in this instance, given that most tradeable databases will be in English.

The Japanese potential in this area remains unclear. It is generally accepted that the whole market for electronically provided commercial information got off the ground later than in Europe, and has been skewed towards the provision of scientific information, rather than towards financial information as has been the case in Europe and the US. In fact, Japan is relatively dominated by foreign databases. In 1985, 82 per cent of databases registered in Japan were developed abroad.

It is difficult to see how that picture will change. Given the software constraints on Japan identified earlier, it can be argued that the development of internationally marketable databases is the ultimate challenge for that country. What is, perhaps, significant is that Japan's financial markets have not yet developed any electronic financial services which even start to challenge the position of the Reuters and the Telerates. This obviously reflects the usual linguistic difficulties, but probably also reflects the slowness with which Japanese financial markets have been liberalised. It is probably not accidental that the world's leading electronic purveyor of financial information is Reuters, which has grown up alongside a London financial market which has been strengthening its position as the world's leading centre for international financial transactions. In so far as the City of London has maintained this status by judicious financial liberalisation, we once again see a link between liberalisation/deregulation and international competitiveness.

The lessons

Given the wide range of activities included in this analysis, generalisations are difficult, however, here are some to stimulate debate.

First, government policies have had a role to play. In Japan, MITI's role in the 1970s clearly helped the Japanese electronics industry to revitalise itself. What is less clear is whether its initiatives in the 1980s will have as great an impact on areas such as software, Fifth Generation computing and so on. The answer is probably not.

Second, the simple judgement that Japan is strong on hardware, weak on software seems to explain a certain amount of the pattern of her successes and relative failures. As indicated above, the jury is still out on the question of whether Japan can overcome its software weaknesses through MITI-led programmes.

Third, European decline is demonstrable through most of the sectors we are discussing. Where spectacular innovations have come (such as

France's Minitel programme), they are normally state-created or state-subsidised. On the other hand, the residual nationalism in Europe is clearly strong enough to hamper companies which now need a continent-wide home market to give them adequate returns on their research and development expenditures.

I am not sure that we have learned any lessons about the alleged damaging effects of the defence-orientation of US and (some) European research efforts. However, what is now clear is that the US Defence establishment is becoming very alert to the alleged national security issues involved in America's growing dependence on Japan for chips, and some other technologies.

Catch-up strategies

This paper started with the assertion that we are only just starting to debate Japan's strengths and weaknesses seriously. The trends in this industry are that Japan should continue to make headway where sheer technical expertise is the key. It remains to be seen precisely how well Japan will actually fare in a world of a permanently strengthened yen, in which software and hardware systems need to be developed simultaneously. However, until evidence actually starts to emerge that Japan is finding the international competition more difficult, Western policy makers have to work on the assumption that they need to improve their policy support of industries that are particularly vulnerable to competition from Japan.

What the arrival of Japan has done is trigger off a wave of defensive collaborative initiatives both within Europe (ESPRIT, RACE, BRITE, EUREKA *et al*) and the US (for example the Microelectronics and Computer Technology Corporation (MCC) and the Semiconductor Manufacturing Technology Institute (SEMATECH)). What needs to be answered is whether these are enough to affect the underlying competitive situation between Japan and these other economic centres.

Since most of these ventures have only existed for a couple of years, if that, there is very little evidence to go on. Within Europe, it could be that the importance of such initiatives is as much psychological as anything else. A number of national champions which have had limited contacts with companies and institutions in neighbouring countries have been given the incentive to find other partners within Europe. At the same time, these programmes may be involving academics more than is usual, thus strengthening the industry-academic bond. The programmes are also carrying out useful work in identifying the need for standardisation in key sectors.

On the other hand, the financial resources offered to these programmes by European governments are not large. One can also raise questions about competition policy. Will Europe ultimately be the winner if potential competitors are in fact encouraged to collaborate with each other?

In fact, despite these governmental initiatives which stress intra-American and intra-European collaboration, there is a strand of corporate strategy which seems to be stressing trans-Atlantic, trans-Pacific or however one describes Euro-Japanese collaboration. The recent Bull-Honeywell-NEC link on computing is perhaps the most extreme of the intercontinental alliances which are being put in place.

At the end of the day, how one improves a country's or continent's competitive position in an industry as complex as this one is a matter for debate. Yes, encouraging collaboration on pre-competitive research may be one way forward. On the other hand, a fierce blast of competition on the more protected parts of this industry may equally have a part to play.

At the end of the day, the most interesting questions are probably no longer about the reasons for Japan's success, but for Europe's relative decline. If, as some have argued, European failure is as much a failure of corporate vision as anything else, should remedies be aimed at the corporate strategists or at the technicians in the reseach laboratories? Do governments actually help by getting involved in trying to stimulate industrial innovation directly, or would they do better by getting out of whole industries, leaving companies to compete openly? Or is there some happy median?

Louis Turner

Mr Turner is the Director of the International Business and Technology Programme of the Royal Institute of International Affairs, in London. He also lectures regularly at the London School of Economics on International Business. He obtained his degree in psychology and philosophy from Oxford University in 1964. A prolific writer, he is the author of nine books, the latest of which is Industrial Collaboration with Japan (Routledge and Kegan Paul, 1987).

The Dynamics of Competition in Information Technology

Warren E Davis

Introduction: factors driving competition

The current state of competition between Europe, the US and Japan in information technology is characterised by rising trade tensions between sovereign participants.

Sanctions remain in place imposed by the US government on Japan for its failure to remove barriers to US semiconductor exports. The EEC has filed a General Agreement on Tariffs and Trade (GATT) case alleging that the US-Japan trade accord on semiconductors is illegal. High-ranking US government officials discouraged the acquisition of America's pioneer semiconductor company, Fairchild, by Fujitsu and dissuaded the Massachusetts Institute of Technology from procuring a supercomputer containing Japanese technology, given the severe trade tensions between the US and Japan in both the semiconductor and computer industries.

These manifestations of tension between leading high-technology trade partners signal instability in the world marketplace. The fall out from this unstable environment is more characteristic of the 'sunset' industries than the 'sunrise' industries: a surfeit of competing firms, towering excess capacity, massive unemployment and operating losses among the major competing firms.

The conditions of competition in the information technology sectors are very dynamic and fluid. The most prominent variable is Japanese industry, moving from a catch up position to market leadership in high-volume commodity memory integrated circuits, presumably a step towards its long-term aspirations to achieve dominance in computers and telecommunications. The Asian surge in information technologies is not limited to Japan. The newly industrialised countries, particularly South Korea and Taiwan, are emulating the Japanese model of developmental capitalism and striving to become world-class competitors in their own right. China will join the fray within a decade or less.

In response, the firms and governments in the US and Europe are searching for a combination of strategies to adapt to the Asian challenge, so as to limit dependency on Asia for information technology by the end of the century and beyond.

The stakes are immense. Some visionaries see the worldwide computer industry growing to shipments of $1 trillion by the year 2000, with telecommunications reaching $300 billion. The above sectors will be increasingly interdependent as computer and telecommunications technologies converge and as semiconductors absorb more systems' functions on a single substrate and rely increasingly on creative embedded software. The information technology sectors are being transformed from several distinct industrial sectors to a single, integrated sector.

At stake in the intensifying world competition is not only the survival, growth and earning power of the several corporate players, but also the national output, export strength, employment level and real incomes of the participating nations.

Facing the issues realistically, we must ask ourselves whether the 40-year American-led era of increasingly open trade under the GATT will endure, or whether in the emerging era of shared economic power among several nations of the free world, a core/periphery model will emerge where a few leaders form a technical elite and the other nations are relegated to dependency status.

Another issue is whether one day Soviet Russia and its East European satellites will be allowed to enter the open market for some information technology products. This development would be based on progress in arms negotiations concerning both nuclear and conventional weapons, settlement of regional conflicts such as Afghanistan and Central America, human rights liberalisation and installation of a market economy in those nations.

In order to gain a better perspective on the future, it is necessary to consider briefly each of the significant factors which are driving world information technology competition. These factors include:
• The role of governments
• The global network of strategic alliances and technological changes
• Corporate strategy and structure
• Precompetitive cooperation among competitors.

The role of governments

Governments are important in shaping the environment for international competitiveness.

In terms of regulatory intervention, the reluctance of several of the
national Post, Telegraph and Telephone Authorities (PTTs) in Europe to
deregulate will mean foregoing new market opportunities in the wake
of the deregulation of American Telegraph and Telephone (AT&T) and
the privatisation of Nippon Telegraph and Telephone Corporation
(NTT). Perhaps the move towards a standardised Integrated Services
Digital Network (ISDN) in Europe will be accompanied by tangible
steps towards deregulation. At the same time, however, the over-
zealous restrictions imposed by the US government on the licensing of
American technology transferred between nations which are members
of the Coordinating Committee for Multilateral Export Controls
(COCOM) impairs the credibility of the marketing efforts of American
information technology companies. Given the widespread availability
or origination of information technology in nations of the West and
other than the US, the only effective way to control unwanted flow of
technology to the Soviet Bloc is to negotiate multilateral control among
all of the COCOM member states.

In terms of standard setting in telecommunications, it is interesting to
note that American telecommunication standards are being set by
large companies rather than the US government. On the other hand,
the Japanese standards are being formulated by the elite bureaux —
based on the national consensus that the standard of excellence in
broadband digital coverage must be of Japanese origin. The
Europeans exhibit heterogenous tendencies, but France employs the
criteria that ISDN standards must enable participation by small companies and individuals. Thus telecommunication standards are being
based on sociological, political and economic considerations as well as
technological ones.

Over and above governments' role in regulation and standard setting,
they pursue explicit or implicit policies for development and growth in
the information technology sector.

In Europe, for several nations, the focus has been to create national
champions serving domestic markets thereby foregoing the scale
advantages of a global market emphasis. There have been institutional
rigidities which have hindered the diffusion of technology and
the mobility of skilled people between research institutes and

universities, on the one hand, and commercial enterprises on the other. The EEC policy of attracting foreign investment with high-technology content and discouraging high-technology imports through high tariffs has not precluded foreign dependency, particularly in microelectronics. Microelectronics simply has not been emphasised by governments, and national champions, like Philips, Siemens, Thompson and SGS, have only recently begun to address this oversight.

The fear of unemployment in Europe seems to have been, to a degree, a self-fulfilling prophecy as absorption by European society of information technologies has lagged far behind the absorption rates in Japan and the US.

Japan has fashioned what Professor Chalmers Johnson of Berkeley, University of California calls 'the miracle of MITI' by attaining fast growth in semiconductors, computers and telecommunications. This has been accomplished first and foremost through tight government control of capital inflows and outflows, control of the banking system, limited foreign access to domestic markets, encouragement of investment allocations to a group of preferred companies in a targeted industry and the organisation of joint research programmes. Corporate managements were obliged to emphasise growth rather than profits or return on investment. In total, these measures socialised the investment risk, inducing individual companies in the favoured sector to over invest, which inevitably leads to over aggressive exports when domestic demand softens. This strategy has been complemented by orchestrated appropriation of foreign technologies (primarily American), carefully dispensed within a rationalised industry so as to induce competition without market confusion.

This close government-industry relationship, plus industry groups and the unique trade associations such as Keidranen, combined with highly efficient volume manufacturing of commodity products and price aggressiveness in world markets, has enabled the Japanese firms to practically rout their foreign competition in certain product areas such as semiconductor memories. The Japanese have not become as dominant in computers because of weakness in software and the inability to set world standards for operating systems. Meanwhile, the Japanese market has remained *de facto* closed to integrated circuit sales by foreign owned companies except for new designs or spot purchases of competitive products. In certain leading edge electronics sectors such as automotive electronics and robotics, foreign semiconductor competitors have simply been 'designed out'.

Unlike all other Organisation for Economic Cooperation and Development (OECD) nations, Japan does not deal in cross-trade of manufactured goods. For example, Germany and France export BMWs and Renaults to each other, respectively; Japan exports Toyotas and Nissans — full stop.

The Japanese brand of explosive growth through developmental capitalism has been emulated by Korea and Taiwan, including a closed banking system and programmed high savings rates. However, Korea and Taiwan lack a major element of the Japanese success model: a large, closed domestic marketplace for developing learning economies prior to export. These newly industrialised countries are also still lagging technologically and are far more dependent on foreign investment and foreign licensing at the current stage of their development than Japan. The Asian Newly Industrialised Countries (NICs) have rapidly converted from rural economies to economies based on manufacturing exports. Their local currencies are linked to the US dollar, giving them an edge in penetrating the US market. The US Government is insisting, however, that these countries revalue their currencies upwards to arrest widening trade surpluses with the US.

The US is the principal market, the technology source, and the advanced education and training base for the Koreans and the Taiwanese. US government officals are leaning hard on the Asian NICs to control their propensity for piracy of foreign intellectual property, from books to cloned IBM personal computers. They are also being pressured to remove their restrictions on foreign imports of information technology products. In addition, they will be pressured to control technology leakages to the Soviet Bloc.

The US has focused its attention on macroeconomics — monetary and fiscal policy and, more recently, exchange rates. Sectoral matters are considered to be in the private domain and subject to the inexorable laws of supply and demand, except in those instances when a corporate crisis threatens the entire economy — Chrysler, Lockheed, Penn Central — and the federal government is obliged to arrange a financial rescue operation. Government research funding is disproportionately allocated to defence and space programmes with regard to private industry. Federal funding of private research has declined despite the ferocity of international competition.

US research efforts have also been impacted by the deregulation of AT&T and the resultant privatisation of Bell Laboratories. The spinning off of Bell has had the unanticipated side-effect of weakening the link between scientific discoveries by the national laboratories and universities, and

SIIT—G

the development of commercial products and processes by private companies. Companies are obliged to rely heavily on equity capital in a volatile institutional equity investment market. Together with a tax policy which favours consumption rather than investment and savings, large defence commitments and social welfare transfer payments — with consequential record federal budget deficits — these factors have led to an increase in the cost of capital, waning productivity and greater dependence on foreign loans.

The Pentagon has formed VHSIC, a government project involving several electronics companies and defence contractor firms, with the objective of channelling commercial know-how into weapon system development. VHSIC is typical of the recent Defence Department R&D model which prescribes development of very complex, highly specialised products. This kind of project is controversial in that some industry observers maintain that it drains scarce scientific and engineering personnel without beneficial commercial fall out of usable know-how.

In Latin America, government-orchestrated development is not following guidelines laid down by other newly industrialising countries. Where Korea and Taiwan, for example, have followed an accelerated industrialisation and export strategy, Brazil and Mexico have fostered an internal development strategy with strict performance requirements and import controls for foreign firms. Using essentially home-grown, 'second-best' technology, Brazil has nevertheless developed an independent minicomputer for domestic use and export, earmarked particularly for other Third World countries.

Strategic alliances and technological changes

While politicians have drawn the competitive lines along sovereign national boundaries and among regional economic blocs, private information technology enterprises have spilled over those boundaries to create an expanding international network of technical alliances. While governments negotiate and subsidise development, foreign companies cooperate with domestic competitors and join international technology networks, all the while competing with increasing intensity.

These represent cross-currents. However, there is an explanation. As technologies merge and sectoral differences blur, markets become global, bridged by digital satellite communication links. As microelectronics move into submicron technologies and creative software emulates human intelligence, technological complexity rises and resource requirements explode — requirements for capital, for know-how and for human expertise. Add to that political barriers which inhibit access to sovereign markets, and the rationale behind international commercial alliances becomes clear. No single sovereign nation and certainly no individual or corporation can accumulate the capital base or the skill pool to dominate the world market in the information era. The nations of the world and their industries are becoming increasingly interdependent. This trend is irreversible and is, in the long term, healthy.

AT&T, using Spanish and Korean off-shore manufacturing bases, forms partnerships with Olivetti and Toshiba to show a European face in Europe and a Japanese face in Japan, as Kenichi Ohmae of McKinsey & Co would phrase it. Intel swaps technology with several European and Japanese firms, while assembling in Malaysia and Singapore. IBM moves to blunt declining market-share in Japan by forming a partnership with Matsushita to compete head on with Fujitsu and Hitachi in the Japanese minicomputer market. Motorola, after being temporarily driven out of the 256K Dynamic Random Access Memory (DRAM) business by underpriced Japanese imports, enters into a partnership with Toshiba to manufacture jointly DRAMs in Japan, while concurrently Motorola joins the SEMATECH consortium of US-owned firms to develop process technologies two or three generations in the future for the 1990s markets.

Another factor favouring cooperation in an environment of conflict and competition is the global automation standards for factory automation (MAPS) and office automation (TOPS), that are potentially applicable worldwide. Whether a given information technology company wants to be a components or materials supplier, a systems manufacturer, or a customer end user, in the future it will have to adhere to the global communications regime or be technologically barred.

Strategy and structure

The information technologies developed in the post-World War Two era are forcing a new manufacturing paradigm based on flexible intelligent systems in all industrialised countries, just as the industrial revolution in the 19th century forced organisations into hierarchical structures accommodating the needs of mass production.

These same information technologies have permitted consumers to enjoy a great diversity of choices in the goods and services they purchase. Dr William Miller, President and Chief Executive Officer of SRI International, observes that instead of economies of need, economies of choice are emerging where individual preference establishes demand — the 'individuation of demand' as he calls it. Organisations must therefore be reconfigured for constant change, or as management consultant Tom Peters describes it, successful firms in the information technology area are 'thriving on chaos', organised to create and exploit constant change.

In this burgeoning information era, all companies in the industrial food chain — suppliers, producers and users — must form deep, intimate linkages to respond to constant variability in design and choice. To continue in the Henry Ford model, arm's length supply chains can cause companies furthest down the 'food chain' to whipsaw out of control.

Technology, particularly the global communications revolution, will cause individual companies to restructure dramatically. Computer-aided Design (CAD), Computer-aided Manufacturing (CAM) and Computer-integrated Manufacturing (CIM) systems will stimulate new horizontal linkages between formerly isolated organisational units. Intermediate management levels will be eliminated as new information will be at the disposal of first-level operators who are better trained and have broader assignments within flexible teams. The absence of first-level foremen at the Toyota/General Motors plant in Fremont, California exemplifies the trend.

Japanese industry is best able to adapt to the new organisational imperative caused by the manufacturing paradigm under information technology. Japanese industrial organisations are tailored to a systems approach, with managerial hierarchies flattened and employees trained to be generalists rather than specialists in dynamic operational teams. This enables Japanese companies to operate corporate-wide systems where design, manufacturing and marketing systems are in a constant but coordinated state of flux; in that environment, management change is the *raison d'être* of the organisation rather than a disruptive factor as is the case in outmoded hierarchical models. There is a downside to the Japanese organisational style. It favours group consensual activity over individual initiative. This atmosphere is not conducive to entrepreneurial innovation.

The US organisations are hampered by several layers of managerial hierarchy and a tendency towards extreme specialisation in job assignments within the office and on the factory floor. The resultant rigidity suffices for very high volume commodity production runs, but will be less efficient for flexible manufacturing to serve constantly changing end-use demand patterns. There is an upside to the American organisational style.

It fosters individuality and a 'management by tension' which continually challenges the conventional wisdom. This atmosphere is conducive to entrepreneurial innovation, and thus to the job mobility and spin-offs to form new ventures.

European companies remain stratified according to social and educational backgrounds, and are hampered by strong unions which participate in management decisions up to the board of directors' level. These conditions tend to inhibit cooperation between suppliers and producers as well as between competitors, and inject inflexibility into individual company operations.

These tendencies are offset by a sound scientific tradition and richly deserved reputation for the manufacture of precision products.

Precompetitive cooperation among competitors

In the last 10 or 12 years, a new phenomenon has emerged with regard to cooperation between competitors. Given the shared power among industrialised nations in technology and market prowess, many nations have put in place programmes to develop their own information technology capabilities thereby limiting dependency on foreign nations as their technology source. Governments have tended to liberalise anti-trust policies and to tap their financial reserves to enable competing companies in a nation, or within an economic union (such as the EEC), to form consortia to conduct joint research and development of critical technologies.

A pioneering consortia of major Japanese electronics companies was formed by Nippon Telegraph and Telephone (NTT) and the Japanese Ministry of International Trade and Industry in the period 1975-79 to conduct research on very large scale integrated circuits. The project focused on the purchase of the latest US semiconductor manufacturing equipment, such as electron beam systems for mask-making systems, for imitation and then refinement to enhance the efficiency and productivity. The resultant production technology was shared by the several participating firms. As a consequence of this single programme, Japanese industry was able to challenge the US' original designs in high-density memory integrated circuits at the 64K (64 000 individual memory calls on a single chip) level of complexity. The rest is history. While the US and European DRAM producers were held at bay and permitted to achieve only trivial sales volumes in Japan, the Japanese companies mounted a major export drive, selling below cost — what could be considered as dumping — where expedient to build up a relationship with foreign electronic equipment manufacturers. Over time they captured over 80 per cent of the world market. The Japanese government contributed a minority share to the costs of the Very Large Scale Integration (VLSI) project, with repayment on that amount deferred until sufficient profits were attained by the participating companies.

Since completion of the VLSI programme, the Japanese government has encouraged and sponsored formation of more advanced information technology research programmes, such as the Fifth Generation Computer Programme. It has also established the Key Technology Centre which is studying advanced process systems, such as compact synchotron light sources for optical lithography, a product five to seven years away from commercial application. Anyone who visits NTT's laboratories at Atsugi must come away convinced that Japan's research programmes cover all important scientific issues at the state of the art automated factory — CAD/CAM, gallium arsenide and large diameter wafers, to name just a few.

In the US and Europe several industry R&D consortia have been formed either on a stand-alone basis or in concert with government.

In the US the first major R&D consortium was the Semiconductor Research Corporation (SRC) founded in 1982 by the Semiconductor Industry Association (SIA). SRC channels industry funds to university research laboratories throughout the country to conduct fundamental microelectronics research and thereby permitting company laboratories to concentrate on shorter term product development. In 1983, a group of computer and semiconductor firms founded the Microelectronics and Computer Development Company (MCC) to develop system architecture, software, methodology and microelectronics capability for computers of the Fifth Generation and beyond.

Under intense competitive pressure from Japan and West Germany in optical lithography and other key processes, the US semiconductor industry is poised to launch a new manufacturing development consortium named SEMATECH, also a SIA initiative. SEMATECH will help fund American advanced equipment development and will establish standards for scale economies in production. It will pool resources from participating firms at a cost of about one per cent of sales (industry already spends 11 per cent of sales on product research). Member companies will appropriate the technology for their proprietary lines and expect to match Japanese manufacturing performance by the mid-1990s.

According to the industry's plan, the US Government, primarily the Defence Department, plus states and local governments, would invest matching funds. The combined industry-government investments would cover the annual cost of $250 million. In addition, to assure an adequate base of fundamental research, the Energy Department's National Laboratories would be given a secondary mission of conducting semiconductor research for commercial use — the first opening of these laboratories since their formation during World War Two.

In Europe, EEC-wide R&D ventures such as European Strategic Programme for R&D in Information Technology (ESPRIT) and EUREKA have been activated during the current decade to lessen dependency on US and Japanese electronics technology — to allow European manufacturers to be part of the core rather than part of the periphery. And quite recently, Philips and Siemens, with support from the Dutch and West German governments respectively, have focused on developing a European capability to produce advanced DRAMs of one megabit and above complexity. To doubly assure access to this technology Philips also licensed DRAM technology from a Japanese source and is becoming a minority shareholder in a new experimental subcontract manufacturing venture in Taiwan which seeks to mass produce DRAMs using the newest Complementary Metal Oxide Semiconductor (CMOS) process techniques. Several European governments, including the French, German and Dutch, are also pooling funds with the information technology industries of several nations to attempt to develop and demonstrate advanced manufacturing systems which can produce micro-miniaturised (.3 micron line width) integrated circuits by the mid-1990s. This project, called JESSI, has objectives and time horizons which are similar to those of the US SEMATECH project.

Summary and conclusions

This paper has attempted to characterise the dynamic universe of international competition in information technology. It has discussed government externalities and regulatory interventions, international strategic technical alliances, the revolution in manufacturing organisation, and the proliferation of joint research and development consortia.

The future opportunities seem limitless, but the problems to resolve along the way appear immense. It is still difficult for American, Japanese, European and Korean semiconductor company executives to be sanguine about future prospects when they absorbed operating losses of $2 billion, $2 billion, $1 billion and $1 billion, respectively, in 1986 alone.

If the upside potential of high growth is to be realised, each country must compromise. America must strengthen linkages between the scientific and education community and its information technology industry — including tapping the National Laboratories and strengthening the educational system — and must also both consolidate and streamline its corporate organisations.

Japan must open its market — not to whistling tea kettles — but to digital switching systems from Siemens or ITT, Video Cassette Recorders (VCRs) from Samsung or Daewoo, microprocessors from Advanced Micro Devices, and supercomputers from Cray Research.

The nations of Western Europe must deregulate PTTs and expand corporate marketing strategies to serve global and regional markets rather than almost exclusively national markets.

The Asian NICs must honour intellectual property rights, ease foreign participation barriers and introduce market research and management control to modulate their frantic expansion programmes. The Latin American NICs must open their borders to allow the diffusion of technology.

All nations must understand, particularly the advanced states, that domestic and international economic and technology policies are inextricably interrelated. They must accept that the global communications revolution is a reality and that it is forcing global interdependence; should they harbour any disbelief, the stock market crash which occurred simultaneously in New York, London, Tokyo, Hong Kong and Australia in 1987 must have removed all trace of that disbelief. While nations must fashion suitable programmes to preserve their unique sovereign interests and cultural heritages, they must also understand that they are all citizens of a smaller earth.

Warren E Davis

Mr Davis' career in the semiconductor industry began in 1969 when he joined Fairchild Camera and Instrument Corporation in a senior staff capacity. For Fairchild, he coordinated projects in strategic planning, international logistics and offshore manufacturing. He joined the Semi-conductor Association in 1978 and is currently Vice President of that Association where he focuses on international trade policy issues. Mr Davis has published several articles on the semiconductor industry, including 'The American semiconductor industry and the ascendancy of East Asia' in California Management Review (1985).

Strategic Alliances and the Government Decision Process

Adrian Norman

Strategic alliances among corporations in the information and telecommunications industries are going to pose problems for decision makers in government, international organisations and business. The corporations in the information and communications industries are making large numbers of strategic alliances, a new name for what at one time we used to call joint ventures. Most of these strategic alliances are cross-national; they are said to give participating companies access to the leading technology or to otherwise closed foreign markets. The US has a technological lead in telecommunications so it is not surprising that there is a strong transatlantic axis to many of the joint ventures, but there are also strong links into the Japanese technology which also has its areas of strength.

Motives for strategic alliances

There are several reasons why there should be so much joint venture activity at this time rather than a decade or two ago. The first reason, of course, is technological change. There are now new ways of doing what used to be done with the old technology, and there are many new things that could not be done at any price with the old technology. Accompanying technological change, there has been a rapid reduction in the cost of individual pieces of equipment, particularly silicon chips, but also of most other high technology inputs. These reductions have been coupled with a very considerable increase in research and development costs. For example, over the last decade the design work on telecommunications central office switches has cost $3 billion in the US, $8 billion in Europe and $2 billion in Japan. The market simply is not big enough to recover costs of that order. It is not surprising therefore that Plessey, Alcatel, Siemens and ItalTel, for example, are coordinating their research and development under the EEC R&D in Advanced Communication Technologies for Europe (RACE) programme.

89

Accompanying the reduction in cost of information technology-based systems and the increase in research and development costs, there has been an evolution towards shorter life-cycles. Today, not only does a telecommunications company have to find a billion dollars to design a new central telecommunication switch, but it has to get its money back in less than 10 years rather than the 25 or even 50 which was available for Strowger equipment. In such an environment, a joint venture begins to sound like a very attractive proposition.

Note that it is not necessry to have a full merger in order to do a joint venture. Joint ventures can apply to any part of the operation from research through development to distribution and marketing. They can cover a small part of one company's product range or embrace everything that several companies do.

One area of joint venture is in the development of standards. In the information technology field, a lot of products are designed in standards committees. Thorn EMI, GEC, Mullard, Philips, Thomson, Siemens and Electrolux are getting together to define standards for the inter-operation of white goods in homes. Standardisation can be very important: imagine the chaos if you were trying to turn on your Philips television using your Siemens telephone and the code was the same as the one which turns on the EMI extinguishers!

Industry over-capacity prevails in many information technology sectors, especially in Europe. It has resulted from national champions being sustained with tax-payers' money to fight for markets which are no longer growing substantially faster than Gross National Product (GNP). When information technology was a very small industry, markets could double in size every year without drawing significant resources away from other sectors of the economy. However, now that half of all economically useful activity in the Organisation for Economic Cooperation and Development (OECD) countries involves the processing of information, the information technology and communications industries cannot grow very much faster than the economies they serve. For some years governments have recognised the importance of information technology industries and, in particular, the role of telecommunications as a mainstay of the economy. They have therefore made substantial investments in their own champion companies, raising awareness of the opportunities and stimulating the customers themselves, and those who invest in them, to pump yet more resources into this sector. As a result, they have succeeded in creating a capacity greater than the markets can absorb. For example, in the telecommunications switching area, it is reckoned that the smallest successful switchmaker needs at least eight per cent of the market, so there is only room for two in the US, two in Europe and one in Japan. The effect of crowding in the market becomes rather clear when even IBM has trouble adjusting to being a supplier of capital goods affected by the investment cycle. Another symptom, of course, is that everybody accuses everybody else of dumping their high-fixed, low-variable cost products in everybody else's markets.

When companies price their products on the assumption that they can succeed in capturing a very large share of the potential market, then obviously those who do not achieve a share sufficient to bring their average cost down close to the marginal cost, are going to lose substantial amounts of money. To achieve these large market shares, suppliers have had to cut costs fiercely, erode prices and compete viciously. This is just what the economics of the free market indicate should happen and, of course, the customers are benefiting.

Indeed, those users of information technology products who do not purchase and apply the most cost-effective technology in the production of other goods quickly find that their costs make them uncompetitive. In countries like Brazil which protect their markets from imports of low-cost information technology products, producers of any range of goods incur higher costs. These producers are then unable to compete in world markets for those goods without selling too low cost. And if they have their debts to pay, then that is what they are forced to do.

The last reason for all the joint venture activity now is the advent of liberalisation and deregulation in the US and UK markets, leading to multi-sourcing of equipment by users and providers of telecommunication services. According to a recent study by the Technical Change Centre in London, the UK telecommunications equipment industry has lost an increasing share of the UK market to foreign companies and failed to make any gains abroad, except in their traditional markets such as the British Commonwealth and the Middle East. The UK companies had reacted by manufacturing more foreign products under licence, so weakening their own product design and their commitment to research and development. UK companies were neither large nor integrated enough to meet international competition and, since they were vulnerable to foreign competitors at any time, they had to aim for success over a much shorter planning cycle.

Corporate strategy, strategic alliances and governments

The objectives of corporations are not the same as those of nations, individuals or international organisations. The objectives of corporations are determined by managers acting within the constraints set by law and by the policies of their owners.

The legal, cultural and social backgrounds of corporations vary within and, even more, between countries. The objectives of the managers of corporations are also a function of culture. In the US, for example, cooperation is almost ruled out by the highly competitive, individualistic and adversarial culture. There are other countries with as many people and as rich in natural resources, but the driving force of this American competitive spirit has powered their economic success. The other side of the coin is revealed by, for example, the rather grudging acceptance of international standards by IBM, the attack by the chief executive of Digital Equipment Corporation on the manufacturing automation protocols developed by General Motors, the withdrawl of Lockheed, Unisys and Allied Signal from the Microelectronics and Computer Technology Corporation (MCC) venture which was set up to help US semiconductor companies to compete with Japan, and the barriers to transborder data flow erected by the Bell system to which international standard modems cannot be connected.

By contrast, the Japanese have a tradition of consensus and a capacity to strive together for a common goal. Any nail whose head sticks up gets hammered down — hardly the right environment for a rugged individualist from the West.

Europeans are very good at cooperating within national boundaries to fight beyond their borders. Our language barriers and differences in legal systems are hard to surmount, but at last we are learning through joint research projects, first to recognise each other's talents and secondly to cooperate to exploit them.

One might expect the differences in national cultures to feed through into differences in managerial objectives but it turns out that there is not much difference in practice. Managers in corporations all over the world are bent on enhancing their business prospects through growth. Dr Walker, in his background paper for the TIDE 2000 (Part 3) Conference in February 1987, proposes several ways in which businesses can enhance their prospects by strategic alliances:
- Access to technology
- Strengthening product portfolio
- Economies of scale
- Access to market
- Sharing of risks and risk reduction
- Combination of resources.

All these turn out to be ways of enhancing growth or of arresting decline. In every corporation anywhere in the world, managers are rewarded for the size of the resources that they manage. All of them are therefore intent on building as large an organisation as possible, where appropriate, by strategic alliances and joint ventures. Whether the owners of the businesses are states, shareholders, banks or foreign corporations, the managerial culture demands growth — particularly in the information technology and communications industries where growth has been rapid and unceasing ever since the industry was founded.

Many powerful corporations can demonstrate substantial benefits from strategic alliances but experience shows that the majority of joint ventures fail. Within the US, for example, where there is no clash of national cultures (although often a clash of corporate cultures), seven out of ten joint ventures (according to Business Week) end in failure. First, the partners find it difficult to put the interests of the joint venture ahead of the interests of their own shareholders. Honeywell, for example, had to look to its shareholders' interests recently and decided to reduce its activities in computing, thereby threatening the success of its joint venture with Bull. To protect itself Bull bought a larger interest in the joint venture. Back in 1981-82, the same companies featured in another shareholders' decision: the French government, in accordance with the principles for which it had been elected, decided to nationalise the computing operations of Bull and buy Honeywell's 47 per cent share. The success or failure of the joint venture was not relevant to these decisions.

In the US the sort of cooperation that is needed for the success of a joint venture is inconsistent with the national culture — the adversarial approach and the emphasis on winning sidetracks the partners and thereby jeopardises the success of a joint venture. Indeed, shareholders would argue that any management that put the interests of a joint venture ahead of the interests of the shareholders was in breach of its duty. Even when there is commitment to the success of the joint venture at top management level, cooperation at lower levels is often difficult and mistrust is endemic. It is noticeable that the same characteristics apply in Europe where the joint venture is international. The European Commission programmes like R&D in Advanced Communication Technologies for Europe (RACE) and EUREKA have been very fruitful in developing mutual trust and respect. Much the same has happened within the Alvey programme in the UK where traditional mistrust between business and academic researchers has been greatly reduced.

In practice, whenever the parties to a joint venture do not agree before the merger on how it should be run, the cultural clash is totally destructive. In the information technology and communications busi-nesses, the success of a merger depends more on the way the human assets increase their effectiveness when brought together than on any advantages that may be gained from bringing physical assets or finances together.

Even if we set aside the 70 per cent of joint ventures which precedent suggests are doomed to fail, the remaining 30 per cent are going to chalk up significant economic successes or will be achieving other objectives sufficiently successfully to justify subsidies from taxpayers' money.

The management ethos which promotes growth and with that the spread of strategic alliances, is not necessarily congruent with the objectives of individuals, nations and international bodies. These objectives are defined in charters, international agreements, laws, treaties, conventions and so on. They are also spelled out in the manifestos of political parties.

National objectives are employment, sovereignty, independence, lack of vulnerability, prosperity, self-esteem and so on. A typical concrete manifestation of such objectives is the way in which French privatisation legislation limits foreign ownership to 20 per cent.

The telecommunications industry has become vital to the effective working of a nation's economy. It has also become very big business in itself, so big in fact that the British government, before privatisation, altered British Telecom's external funding limit — the amount of money they could borrow from the government — in line with national macro-economic policy, not with the needs of the business.

The European telecommunications supply industry, which had been stable for the better part of a century, is now crumbling under technical, economic and political forces. The maintenance of a monopoly supplier of telecommunications services is seen by some countries as a national objective, supporting social, political and economic goals, not simply those objectives appropriate to a business. The economic cost of achieving social and political goals through such monopolies has caused a reduced GNP growth rate in Europe of about 0.5 per cent to a one per cent compound over the past 30 or more years. Without it, the average GNP per capita in Europe today would be a third higher.

The continental Post, Telegraph and Telephone Authorities (PTTs) (whose most useful monopoly has been of the ear of the government through which advice on telecommunications strategy can be delivered), now see such developments as the Integrated Services Digital Network

(ISDN) as a way of sustaining their cartels. Some of their biggest customers see it as a means of bypassing the expensive links whose tariffs have been set in favour of the voter rather than of business.

At the same time, governments and corporations are worried about their dependence on other nations, however reliable allies they may have proved to be in the past. The US Department of Defence, for example, is worried about the Japanese lead in semiconductors and is proposing a US joint-venture programme to strengthen the commercial semiconductor industry which underpins the military one. European governments and companies are concerned about the extra-territorial application of US law and the interpretation of the Coordinating Committee for Multilateral Export Controls (COCOM) regulations which enable the US government, rather than the government of the pertinent NATO partner, to determine where certain products and services may be sold. When British Telecom and McDonnell Douglas planned a joint venture to provide network services to European customers, many of the latter were reluctant to use the service because the data would be switched within the US where the US courts had legal jurisdictions.

Pressure from well-organised supplier lobbies makes governments act to protect existing jobs, markets and access to attractive contracts for their own country's firms; for example, UK suppliers and unions protested when Mercury Communications plc bought Northern Telecom's DMS 100 and British Telecom bought APT's 5ESS-PRX switches. When Siemens bid for CGCT, in answer to an invitation from the French government who wished to privatise the company that had been nationalised in 1981-82, the US threatened to impede Siemens' sales to the regional Bell operating companies.

Thus, decision makers must use their limited powers to safeguard these other interests while getting the benefit of strategic alliances between corporations. Just so long as these alliances are responses to competitive pressures rather than devices to protect monopolies or cartels, global economic welfare will be increased. There will, of course, be advantages and disadvantages at every level of economic unit below that of the world as a whole. Nevertheless, in almost every case users will become better off even when particular suppliers in particular countries are the losers.

As an analytical observer, however, one must keep in mind that governments are not necessarily in the business of maximising total wealth, either global or national. They and those that vote for them are

SIIT—H

usually more concerned with maximising their share of total wealth. They also want to maintain their power to determine the course of events and to be in control of their own destiny.

Decision makers and the spread of information technologies

In reality, however, the powers of decision makers in governments and international organisations are limited. First, there is no way that they can repeal the laws of physics. ASTRA, the consortium planning Luxembourg's medium-powered satellite, will be broadcasting into France and Germany, and French and German citizens will be pointing their receiving dishes at it. The national telecommunications authorities will have no way of stopping such reception equipment from being used and it is almost certainly contrary to the European Convention on Human Rights to try to do so. Freedom of information and communication is likely to be upheld, unless such freedom can be shown to threaten somebody else's rights to communicate. Since any information can be converted to digital form and then stored on a wide variety of media, there is nothing governments can achieve by regulating the use or movement of any one medium. Nowadays one can store several megabytes of information on a plastic card and send it through the post to circumvent a regulatory body which tried to prevent the movement of the same information over a telecommunications link. At the time of the Iranian revolution about a decade ago, the Shah's government tried to prevent Ayatollah Khomeni from gaining access to the broadcasting media. Instead Khomeni organised the distribution of his speeches on cassettes which could be played on tape recorders. One will note the similarities to the development of the television network in Italy where government regulations banned chains of transmitters linked by cables. Burlesconi responded by moving video tapes to the autostrada and thereby evading the prohibition on nationwide broadcasting.

Even if the powers of decision makers were not limited, some of the objectives that they are trying to achieve simultaneously are inherently incompatible; for example, protecting the rights of copyright holders and facilitating the transfer of knowledge to students. Teachers and civil servants happily copy copyright works in the interests of their students or to improve the flow of information within government.

Even when decision makers achieve the right balance in the general interest, it is quite likely that they will be removed from office by their constituents, shareholders or governments who do not wish to sacrifice their particular interests. Decision makers must therefore use the powers they do have as effectively as possible. The first requirement, of course, is to understand the problem, not just part of it. To treat an issue as purely economic, social, political or legal is not effective. In particular, it is essential for decision makers in government and international organisations to understand thoroughly the capabilities and limitations of new information technologies. Nobody afraid to tackle the technical issues should be regarded as fit to tackle the social, political or economic ones. After all, the technical issues are the easy ones. A clear understanding is what is needed and it is relatively easier to gain a good background in information technology and telecommunications than to be a systems designer or telecommunications engineer.

Decision makers also have to understand the solutions that are open to them and to the others involved. This means studying other people's perceptions of what the issues are, where their constituencies are, who they represent, what kinds of conclusions are acceptable to those that vote for them and so on. It is important to note, for example, that the US cannot enter into certain kinds of agreements which would require it to bind the individual states. No British government can bind its successor since in the UK, parliament rather than the courts is sovereign. For example, the present British Tory government cannot guarantee to a foreign partner in a joint venture that a future Labour government would not nationalise the British partner.

Decision makers need to amplify the power available to them by appropriate alliances, by pre-emptive moves, by the appropriate choice of secrecy and publicity, by trading one objective for another, and particularly by choosing the ground on which the decisions will be taken. One of the most important powers which may be available, or denied, to a particular decision maker is the choice of forum in which to negotiate. The other party may have brought the matter up in a forum not of a decision makers' choosing, or the particular issue may be packed with a set of other issues, one of which might be very much more important. In such situations the interests of weaker parties often get lost. The US, for example, is taking a number of regulatory issues to the General Agreement on Tariffs and Trade, while several other countries are trying to have the International Telecommunications Union's World Administrative Radio Conference address trade issues. Other parties to these discussions are trying to stop them from doing so.

Within the European Commission there is pressure to move some of the decisions about telecommunications into a forum dominated by the users of telecommunications rather than the suppliers. Customers are looking for tariffs that more closely reflect the costs of the new technologies which are now available, whereas suppliers are looking to milk the maximum revenue from past investments in order to be able to meet social as well as economic goals.

Another device available to decision makers is to create artificial distinctions which permit the introduction of new local rules to promote or discourage new entrants into the marketplace. The distinctions between value-added network services, enhanced services, managed networks and packet networks, and between customer premises equipment and network terminating equipment are the stuff of theology rather than technology and economics.

Several European governments treat equipment purchases by their PTTs under the government procurement codes so that they are exempted under the General Agreement on Tariffs and Trade (GATT). The US is organising its Department of Defence to procure research and development from potential commercial semiconductor companies so that they can reduce the cost of development of new, competitive random access memory chips. The Department of Defence argues that a powerful domestic semiconductor industry is necessary to keep it ahead of its enemies.

Another trick open to some decision makers is to employ all the experts in the field and thus maintain a monopoly of the sources of advice to the government. There are those that argue that the most significant monopoly of the Deutsche Bundespost is the monopoly of the ear of the government.

Finally, of course, the decision maker in one country can team up with the national favourite in another country and thus get access to the government's ear. At the time of the preparation of the UK Data Protection Act the American banks in London invited the British Home Secretary to lunch to explain the importance of appropriate legislation to the success of commercial operations in the City of London. This particular lobbying exercise was actually organised by a British group anxious to see the passage of suitable legislation. The British group had recognised that foreign commercial enterprises were likely to have greater influence than their British counterparts.

To sum up, clearly strategic alliances among corporations in the information and telecommunications industries do pose problems for decision makers. These problems stem from the incompatibility of the objectives of corporations, governments and international organisations.

The powers of decision makers are limited, but they have to use their power effectively to understand its limitations and all the dimensions of the issues with which they are dealing, not only from their own point of view, but also from the point of view of all other parties involved.

Adrian Norman

Mr Norman is Senior Management Sciences Consultant in the London office of Arthur D Little. For three years, from 1980-83, he was seconded to the UK Cabinet Office, initially to the Central Policy Review Staff and then to the Information Technology Unit, which he helped to set up. In addition, Mr Norman has represented the UK at the OECD, both as a delegate to the Information, Computers and Communications Policy Committee, and as the UK's designated expert on transborder data flows. He is also the author of several books and many articles on information technology, its applications and implications.

PART IV

Information Technology and Developing Countries

While developed countries now reap the benefits from information technology, the majority of the world's population, which lives in developing countries, has hardly come into contact with it. Information technology will soon enter their societies and will offer both a threat and an opportunity for development.

Information technology can be considered to be a threat because its spread may lead to technological recolonisation or over-dependence. Developing countries are forced to import technology from the developed countries; hardly able to catch up, they will keep running behind the ever faster and more technologically advanced developed world.

On the other hand, greater productivity, the spread of information and wider educational possibilities may provide developing countries with the unique opportunity to leap-frog, that is short-cut the time of economic development. Whole stages of economic or technological development may be left out, allowing these nations not only to catch up, but even potentially to bypass the developed world.

How these opportunities and threats are handled depends mainly upon decision makers in the Third World. The diffusion of information technology is a technical and a financial question, but it is even more so a political question. It is incumbent upon decision makers to allow information technology to work to the benefit of all and not simply to the advantage of a small elite. Information in all organisations relates to power and its distribution, therefore, implies power sharing. Emphasis must be placed on human resources development and leaders should question whether old ways of thinking or functioning are good guides for the future.

Information Technology as a Threat and an Opportunity

Shaozhi Su

Information technology's impact on the developing countries is a complex and multifaceted topic. First, information technology is a term which aggregates a number of new technologies including electronics, computer hardware and software, robotics, computer-aided design and manufacture, fibre optics, optical instruments, communication equipment, photovoltaic technology, biogenetics and yet other new inventions. Although they influence one another considerably, these technologies cannot be easily compartmentalised because different technologies have a different impact on the economic growth of the developing countries.

Second, the developing countries, or what are often called the Third World countries, are not a homogeneous entity. There are those which are comparatively developed and those which are comparatively backward. Almost all of these countries share some common characteristics, yet they significantly differ in many respects; thus, information technology will not have an identical impact on the economic progress of any two of them.

Always keeping these two factors in mind, this paper will address specific issues at stake in the analysis of information technology's effect on developing countries.

The options: development versus absorption

Developing countries can no longer afford to ignore the technological revolution but have to put on the agenda the development of new technologies and their own industrialisation. There are essentially two approaches — one based on an internal industrial and technological revolution or one based on the absorption and efficient application of new technologies from abroad.

IV: IT and Developing Countries

In order for a developing country to forge ahead with the first approach — that of a technological revolution — that nation needs an appropriate background for such an effort to be successful.

First, there must be an adequate educational, as well as scientific, level. It is required for the mastering of various technologies and for supporting technological development.

The nation should have available substantial funding for research and development, for the training of personnel, the study of technological inventions and the extensive popularising of their application.

Large, rational organisational agencies and economic bodies should be in place and ready to initiate large-scale research, to promote the development of new technologies and to spread their use. The 'organisation ware' should also be in place, that is to say that there should be the systematic research and design of policies, and management and organisational structures suited to the application of new technologies.

Technology must become an internal self-operating factor in the socio-economic process, and a related component in the internal motivating force of a country. Technological advance, once begun, promotes scientific, educational, cultural, economic and social development and quickens the accumulation of material wealth.

A democratic and open society is essential, especially today when the rapid development of information technology has increased the economic, political and cultural contact among nations, and when a highly centralised and closed society does not suit the needs of the new technological revolution.

More often than not developing countries do not have the resources or the institutional structures, described above, which make an internal technological revolution possible.

The only alternative to the internal creation of new technologies is the absorption of technology from abroad. Historically, all the major inventions capable of inducing a technological revolution came from the developed countries. This is particularly true of the current new technological revolution centred around microelectronics. These technologies come from countries with a vastly different social, economic and cultural environment making effective transfer difficult. Yet, such an approach can be successful if certain conditions are met.

Modern technologies must be absorbed, digested and enhanced. A first criteria in this respect is the advancement of the general educational and cultural level, quantitatively as well as qualitatively.

In addition, the developing nation must adopt proper policies and create institutions which serve to heighten popular interest in acquiring and disseminating advanced knowledge and technologies, and which provide the necessary material conditions for drawing on new technologies. These include a relevant infrastructure so that, through investment, technologies can be converted into products and the cycle of the commercialisation of technological findings can be shortened.

Again, such a society should be an open one. Measures should be adopted to extend democracy within the country, stimulate the economy and open the nation to the outside world. In absence of these conditions, it will be impossible to assimilate — let alone put to good use — advanced technologies even when there is strong foreign financial and technical assistance.

It must be added that while appropriate domestic policies are most important for developing countries, it is obviously inadequate to depend exclusively on domestic research and development. In order for them to absorb and digest advanced technologies such measures must be accompanied by the acquisition of advanced technologies through a system of international cooperation — a comparatively rational system allowing for the convenient and inexpensive transfer of technologies.

The desirability of introducing new technologies

An important corollary to the question of whether developing countries can effectively absorb advanced technologies is the question of whether such a step is desirable. New technologies, being neutral by themselves, can be used for a variety of purposes, good or bad, and they can have a variety of influences, favourable or unfavourable.

In general, the adoption of new technologies has an overall impact on the economic, political and social aspects of a given society, involving, for instance, economic growth, efficiency, the employment level and structure, income management, a change in the requirements for particular human skills and capabilities, a shifting of regional economic activity, a change in the structure of world trade, and an intensification of international competition.

IV: IT and Developing Countries

In the context of North-South relations, advanced science and technology, which are usually research, capital or knowledge intensive, have made the North superior to the South. What worries the developing countries most is the danger that, despite their best efforts, they will lag increasingly behind the developed countries and become more and more dependent on them for technological know-how.

These worries are not without foundation. Most of the developing countries have an economy which suffers from a surplus labour force. Poverty and underdevelopment often give rise to persistent and enormous unemployment and underemployment. As it is, the employment situation is fairly susceptible to the impact of new technologies. In particular, microelectronics and other technologies with labour-displacing tendencies, are likely to make more people lose their jobs.

Even if the introduction of these technologies does not cause more unemployment, their introduction will change the composition of the labour force. For instance, the necessary expansion of the ranks of scientists, engineers, high-level technicians and skilled machine operators will reduce the need for technically inferior workers in the section of the workforce engaged in manual labour. Because the developing countries often have a comparatively low educational and cultural level, it is usually difficult for their people to shift from jobs requiring only a low technical level to those calling for greater skills. New technologies, thus, may entail more unemployment. In the end, increased unemployment and the changed composition of the labour force will widen the income gap in the developing countries.

A second new factor to consider is that since the developed countries can update their mature industries by using new technologies, it is no longer necessary for them to move such industries to the developing countries. This will begin to delay the industrial shift from the former countries to the latter ones. As a result, the pace of industrialisation in developing countries will suffer.

Third, by applying technologies to the manufacture of new products, the developed countries will begin to use new materials or will save energy or raw and semi-finished materials. Being research and knowledge intensive, the new products manufactured will carry a high value added. This means not only that there will be a widening ratio of exchange between manufactured and primary goods, but also that the economies of the developing countries which chiefly depend on the export of farm and mineral products as well as raw materials, will be seriously disadvantaged.

Cheap labour has been one of the strengths of the developing countries when competing on the world market. With new technologies, especially microelectronics and robotics, this advantage will be lost.

For instance, due to production savings from cheap labour, these countries have been very competitive in the labour-intensive textile industry. However, the developed countries will increase their effort in research and development and will expand the use of computer software. These developments, together with the integration of innovative electronic automisation, will enable the whole textile industry to become a subsector of the high-technology industry. As such, differences in the cost of labour will cease to be a decisive factor in the total cost of production, thereby weakening the international competitiveness of the developing countries. The same will be true of the garment industry, the testing and assemblage sector of the semiconductor chip industry, the manufacture of software and even the automobile industry.

Because of what has been described above, it is unavoidable that the differences between the North and the South in technology, unemployment and income will increase.

Nonetheless, we cannot say that the developing countries cannot benefit from modern technologies, especially biotechnology and the use of solar energy. Easy to utilise, biotechnology helps tap the potentials of agriculture and aids in the development of medicine. It also helps increase grain production and save chemical fertiliser. Take an example from South America where a computer-aided research project for the improvement of a strain of corn seed yielded direct and indirect benefits. Output was increased by three to four times.

Another case in point is that of microelectronics which can enable production and services to operate on a smaller scale and in a scattered way, thereby allowing the developing countries to avoid the undesirable side-effects which the developed countries experienced in the early stages of their industrialisation.

In a word, the new technologies present a provocative challenge to the developing countries while simultaneously making them more technically dependent on the developed countries. To avoid or minimise this dependency, countermeasures or counter-policies should be taken.

1 The developing countries must raise their educational level, strengthen the basic sciences and their research capability, and

heighten their scientific and technological level so as to increase their productive capacity.

2 The import of new technologies should not be overemphasised as traditional and conventional technologies are still important for developing countries. They should, instead, adopt technological pluralism. That is to say, they should integrate all types of technologies, from traditional to the most sophisticated, in order to increase their productive forces. There should, of course, be some pre-conditions for the adoption of technological pluralism. For instance, there should be a deep understanding of the characteristics of traditional technologies and production methods so that the areas where new technologies can be best integrated can be identified with great accuracy. The transfer of technology to the productive parts of the economy should be encouraged; and, to facilitate the integration of new and traditional technologies, it is necessary to build the relevant infrastructure and produce appropriate software.

3 The developing countries need to create jobs to counteract the menace of unemployment caused by the introduction of new technologies.

4 Due to the interdependent nature of the world economy, it is imperative to improve the conditions for 'North-South' negotiations and enhance 'South-South' cooperation with the purpose of fostering international cooperation in new technologies and improving conditions for technology transfer.

China and the new technologies: related problems and countermeasures

As the author pointed out at the TIDE 2000 (Part 2) Conference in Honolulu, Hawaii, in May 1986, 'the scientific and technological revolution represents both an opportunity and a challenge' for China.

China has done well in scientific and technological development. It has been impelled by its current reforms in the economic structure, in science and technology management, in systems and education, in its open-to-outside-world policy, in its policy towards the intellectuals and in its import of advanced technologies.

China's production of computers has rapidly increased. In 1986, it turned out 240 small, medium and large computers, a 16 per cent increase over

1985; the number of microcomputers manufactured reached 32 600, an 18 per cent increase over the preceding year. Computer networks are playing an ever more important role in schools, factories, government offices and hospitals. By mid-December 1986, China's export of electronic products had risen to the value of 113 million US dollars.

There has also been swift growth in China's space industry which has become a vanguard of the Chinese economy. It has yielded beneficial economic results by stimulating the development of other new technologies in the country and by producing many spin-offs in other economic sectors. China has drawn upon the advanced achievements which the United States and the Soviet Union have made in space technology, but the ratio of investment to production in its space industry is now higher than that in both these countries. Of all industries, the space industry shows the narrowest margin between China's present stage of development and the most advanced world standards. Exports accounted for 9.5 per cent of the total output value of China's space industry. As reported, China has signed contracts with the United States and Sweden for the launch of their satellites in 1988. Quite clearly, rapid growth of the space industry is encouraging in a country which traditionally exports labour-intensive, agricultural, textile and other light industrial products.

Despite these clear developments, China's relative 'computer wealth' in the information industry is rather feeble when compared with the US and some of the other advanced countries. China is still weak in the number of powerful mainframe computers in use, or if its support capabilities are compared to the millions of lines of operating systems and software applications, or to the amount of programme analysts and designers, at work in other countries.

Based upon Soviet technology, imported into the country in the late 1950s, the indigenous Chinese computer industry is now developing technically from the Third to the Fourth Generation. This means that it is one generation behind the US and Japan. Estimates reveal that China's information industry has developed to a fair extent in the 1980s. When compared with the rapid growth of the US electronics industry, however, it is lagging further and further behind the world's advanced standards due to a weak foundation and inadequate funds. As a point of comparison, the US electronics industry quadrupled in total output value during the decade 1975-84, registering an annual growth rate of 16.8 per cent. In recent years, it has grown even more rapidly.

Results from the completion of its Sixth Five-Year Plan (1981-85) indicate that China invested a great deal in its electronics industry and imported a lot of electronic products during that period, but with no significant effect, especially in terms of computer application. Some reports show that only 20-30 per cent of its total number of computers were in regular use during the period of the Sixth Five-Year Plan. This was an appalling waste.

China has not yet been able to put its computers to full and rational use. In recent years, an urge to rationalise and streamline management and operations has led to the import of a large number of computers from the US, UK, Japan, France and Australia. Yet it lacks adequate knowledge for their effective use and has no unified planning.

Moreover, undue importance has been given to the acquisition and development of hardware at the expense of software, which is today increasingly regarded as being a strategic resource.

No huge contingent of computer-using personnel is available. China has its own personnel-training plan. Its plan for the 1982 census included the training of software and hardware personnel, as well as data entry staff. With UN assistance, a National Computer Centre was set up under the State Statistical Bureau, using IBM mainframes and the Wang data communication networks which were built in all of the regional sub-centres. The census-taking, itself a colossal task, needed 100 000 Chinese personnel trained in the principal computer techniques. Unfortunately, the majority of them could only do the relatively mechanical job of data entry, which meant that there was, and still is, an acute shortage of people capable of using computers.

The biggest problem facing China is its present failure to integrate information technology with production, a process which can play the role of a multiplier in the development of a modern economy. The transformation of research findings into productive capacity proceeds at a very slow pace.

Paramount importance should, therefore, be attached to the use of computers and to the multiplying role information technology can play in the modern economic system. In its Seventh Five-Year Plan (1986-90), China recognises the development of the traditional industries as a strategic priority in line with the specific conditions in China.

As it is, traditional industries have grown into industries equipped with information technology. The modern economy is entering a stage marked by intensive agriculture and automised factory and office work. As a consequence, modernisation of traditional industries and attainment of economic development objectives will be out of the question without information technology. It is predicted that, in the next few decades or so, information technology will play a role in economic development which will gradually become more important than that presented by energy and materials — it will become a pillar of economic growth.

The challenge of a new technological revolution is, first of all, the challenge of information technologies. The 'motor' of such a revolution is computers in particular. A protractedly backward information technology will deprive the economy of the capacity for sustained growth. It is possible for China to grasp the opportunity offered by the current technological revolution. The best way to achieve this is to utilise fully modern information technology so that, in economic development, China can get multiplied results and speed up the transition from the traditional model to a technologically advanced one. We cannot wait for the growth of traditional industries and then follow it with development in information technology, because this will mean a loss of time. China needs to assess the beneficial role which information technology can play in economic development and thereby accelerate the growth of the information industry — this is the most important way to pick up the challenge of the new technological revolution.

In consideration of the factors outlined above, China plans to take the following measures:

1 *Transform traditional industries with new technologies, and foster the development of systematic and concerted scientific and technological capabilities*
As was said previously, one of the strategic priorities of China's Seventh Five-Year Plan is to expand its traditional industries which, at present and for a considerably long time, will be of vital importance to the country. For the technical transformation of such industries, efforts will be made to develop new technologies internally, as well as to assimilate and master the imported ones in this five-year period. China expects to supply traditional industries with advanced and suitable technologies and equipment, including high technologies.

China will readjust the priorities at the existing research institutions to meet the new requirements, or will set up new institutions which are capable of systematically and concertedly absorbing and further developing imported technologies so that they can serve such basic economic sectors as energy, transportation and materials; they will also aid in the technical transformation of those traditional industries which are technically weak. In the manufacture of the means of

SIIT—I

production or of consumption, great efforts will be made to introduce new technologies with a view to increasing the competitiveness of the products on both domestic and international markets.

2 *Develop new technologies on a selective basis to help create new industries*
China will emphasise developing microelectronics (informatics and telecommunications included) and biotechnology capabilties during the Seventh Five-Year Plan. During this period, it is anticipated that China will witness a notable advance in these fields through the concentration of our human, material and financial resources.

Special attention will be paid to developing new technologies and making them serve industries. Research institutions will be encouraged to cooperate, or even merge with the relevant industrial enterprises, in order to build a number of technology-intensive industries that possess substantial productive capacities, and are capable of rapidly assimilating, applying and developing the imported technologies.

3 *Make substantial efforts to develop and spread readily implementable and easily reproducible technologies that can serve growing local industries*
Beginning with the Seventh Five-Year Plan, China has begun to implement the 'Spark Plan' for technological development, designed to promote the growth of local industries. The plan is to stimulate the technical progress of township enterprises and lead to the effective integration of modern science and technology into these businesses. Expanding such enterprises is of great significance to China's economic and social development. By the end of 1984, their gross output value had reached more than 17 per cent of total Chinese industry and agriculture, and more than 24 per cent of total Chinese industry. Meanwhile, these enterprises are offering an opportunity to solve China's problem of surplus rural labour by creating large numbers of jobs for peasants. Statistics compiled up to the end of 1984 show that more than 30 million peasants were employed by Chinese township enterprises. Also, the building of small towns around the township enterprises can help avoid problems of urbanisation, and thus provide an example for the future modernisation of China's rural areas.

4 *Step up the growth of educational as well as research and development efforts*
China will make enormous investments in education, in personnel training and in scientific research and development projects. Emphasis

will be placed upon the use of modern information technology in these respects. At the same time, efforts will be intensified to strengthen basic, applied and technical research which can exert a profound and far-reaching influence on the growth of the national economy.

5 *Persist in opening to the outside world and work for better international cooperation*
China's actual conditions determine that it cannot develop new technologies by exploring methods alone or by starting from scratch. Thus, China will persist in opening to the outside world and, under a unified plan, in introducing from abroad advanced technologies and managerial expertise, as well as funds and qualified personnel. Measures should be taken to integrate closely the imported technologies with the country's key research projects and coordinate fruitfully such technologies with the enterprises' technical forces, all for the purpose of creatively applying and then adding to the imported know-how.

The world economy is an integrated whole, and China is always ready to increase cooperation with other countries in science and technology. Growing friendship and cooperation among nations not only serve the interests of the parties concerned, but also contribute greatly to peace and development all over the world.

Shaozhi Su
Professor Su is a Research Professor at the Chinese Academy of Social Sciences, Professor at the Graduate School of CASS, and former Director of the Institute of Marxism-Leninism-Mao-Zedong Thought. His publications include: 'Democratization and reform' (Beijing, People's Daily Press, 1987), in Chinese; 'Socialism in the contemporary world' (Beijing, Guangming Daily Press, 1985), in Chinese; and 'Marxism in China', with others (Nottingham, Spokesman, 1983), in English.

Information Technology and Developing Countries: Implications for Decision Makers

Jonathan Parapak

We are now living in a new era — the era of information. The future is exciting because of the tremendous progress that is being made in this area. We are enjoying the benefits brought about by information and communications technology, and look forward to further developments in the technology and the positive effects that these will have on the quality of life. Unfortunately, the benefits of this progress can so far be enjoyed by only a small percentage of the world's population. While we converse about the future of information technology, millions are still waiting their turn to obtain a telephone. While we experience the excitement of a video teleconference, millions are still deprived of even a black and white television set. In other words, we cannot refer to the future of information and communications technology and international decision makers without also considering the situation in the developing countries.

Looking at the implications for decision makers of the future progress of information and communications technology, one can ask 'Who are the decision makers under consideration?'. One often thinks of the decision makers who are in managerial positions in government, commerce and industry and one tends to neglect the non-formal decision makers in our societies. I submit, therefore, that we should really be concerned with the whole spectrum of decision makers in our society, both formal and non-formal leaders in our communities. The religious sector, the media and the educational community, among others, make up the non-formal sector of decision makers whose influence over the general public is often unnoticed or under-estimated.

The progress of information and communications technology

It is not the author's intention to review the long history of the progress of this technology but rather to draw attention to the incredible progress which has taken place during the last 30 years. During that short period man has seen unimaginable advancement in the field of electronics, from the creation of discreet transistor components to very large-scale integration. There has been fantastic progress in computers from a single function to intelligent computers. There has been progress in conventional telecommunications services and the exponential growth of value-added services, made possible through the integration of computers and communications. There has been progress in transmission technologies in the area of satellite systems, submarine cables and optical fibres. One can read about information network systems in Japan and the experimental wired cities in some industrial countries. These are indications of the tremendous progress in terminal equipment technology which has ushered man into the almost unlimited area of value-added services.

If one tries to see the future orientation of information and communications technology, one could expect:

1 Greater and greater integration of computer and communications technology which will enable companies to offer virtually any service required by the public.

2 An increasing demand for flexibility both in services and in capacity utilisation. The current trend of modularity which allows the integration of many different products to perform new tasks, will continue.

3 An increasing use of optical fibre technology both for terrestrial links as well as submarine links complementing the use of satellite links for broadband services.

4 An increasing demand for earth terminals for satellite communications located on customers' premises which will form an 'information highway' for direct use by the customers. Such a situation may require new technology offering cost savings and flexibility.

Information and communications technology in the developing world

As noted by the Maitland Commission of the International Telecommunications Union (ITU), out of the 600 million telephones in the world today over three-quarters are concentrated in nine advanced industrial countries. Almost all the telecommunications equipment is manufactured in the industrial countries. In most of the developing countries the telephone densities are still below 10 line units per 100 inhabitants, and, in fact, in some countries of Asia and Africa the density is less than one per 100 people. For the transmission of telegraphic and telex messages and data, Arthur D Little estimates that the North American market will be 60 times larger than the African market and 30 times larger than the Latin American market by 1990.

The general picture is about the same if one looks at computer utilisation. Mainframe installations in most developing countries are still very few. Personal computers have only appeared during the last five years and the volume of sales is still low. For example, in Indonesia where there is a population of 165 million people, only around 20 000 personal computers were sold last year.

When looking at the statistics, it should be kept in mind that the countries of the Third World are a highly diverse and largely fragmented group. Information technology has not had, and will not have, a uniform impact upon them. For some, there are problems so fundamental that, at best, they can be selective users of information technology. In some cases, the economic situation during the last years has not only not improved but has worsened, falling to pre-1970 levels. These countries have huge grain output deficiencies, are overpopulated despite high infant mortality rates, disease and low life expectancy, have high illiteracy rates and low educational and skills levels. Any progress is hampered by inadequate infrastructures, marginal governmental efficiency, the lack of industry and the fact that most of these countries are only barely integrated into the international economic system. The term 'vicious circle of poverty' aptly describes their plight.

In other developing countries, the basic problems of production have been solved and the primary challenge is to continue economic growth and technological development. Information technology will be a primary catalyst in their drive for economic progress. There are problems, however, and greater diffusion and application of information technologies will be crucial.

For all developing countries, the present low penetration of information and communications technology is due to several factors, which include the following:

1 Communications and information technology is still practically 100 per cent imported from the industrial countries, requiring a considerable amount of already scarce foreign exchange. There is, thus, a major gap between the need for information technology and the capacity to purchase hardware, software and services.

2 There is a shortage of skilled manpower. Technological and managerial expertise is still in the development stage, necessitating technical and management aid from the industrial countries.

3 While industrial countries are concentrating on developing and creating fully automatic and high capacity systems to exploit fully the economic benefits of the new technology, developing nations are struggling with job creation for the millions who are unemployed and with the provision of basic services in rural areas.

4 For many countries there are conflicting objectives. For example, to become reasonably self-reliant, the nation must invest in science and technology. At the same time, it must invest in productive activities to generate income and welfare. In telecommunications, R&D activities must be promoted and supported without letting the fundamental need for a more efficient and high-quality telephone service fall by the wayside.

5 There is also the need to attract foreign capital investment and venture capital to support growth. Yet, local entrepreneurs and businesses which are the best guarantee for technological independence should not be placed at a disadvantage in competing against larger foreign firms in their own markets.

6 Greater coordination at the international level is necessary. Yet, due to the present world political environment there appears to be limited interest in the international community in investing additional time and money in economically unstable countries which are already overloaded with foreign debt.

In spite of the problems outlined above, there is relatively rapid progress in some areas. Some countries have introduced domestic and regional satellite systems. Digital technology, as the basis for computer communications integration, has been implemented in some parts of the national network. Optical fibre is beginning to find its way into the transmission networks of some of the developing countries.

Application of modern technology — Indonesia's experience

The developing world could actually 'leap-frog' over stages in the development process by taking advantage of the benefits of modern technology. Indonesia took the very brave and important decision about

10 years ago of implementing a national domestic satellite system, which was seen as a cost-effective way to provide telecommunications services, television, radio and other services to remote areas or between largely separated regions.

The system was constructed and ready for service in a very short time, and is capable of serving the needs of the whole country for television and other communications services. The impact has been phenomenal. The system has contributed significantly to the integration of the people and the country within the context of the 'archipelagic outlook'. It has helped to open new horizons in education, to integrate the country's economy, and to open new isolated areas for oil and mining activities, and trade and industry, as well as for tourism. Today the system is operating nearly 200 earth stations for public telecommunications as well as many others for television reception and/or military applications.

Digital technology is also gaining momentum in Indonesia. Several digital exchanges are operational both for domestic and international services. The first optical fibre cables are used in the telecommunications network, preparing Indonesia for offering integrated services.

Why did Indonesia choose to establish a domestic satellite system? It recognised several advantages of the system, such as:

1 The large coverage, which could be tailored to suit a large country like Indonesia which has almost 10 million square kilometres of land and over 165 million people.

2 The access techniques which allow the efficient use of satellite capacity for light route interconnectivity.

3 The relatively short implementation period (less than two years).

The process was a very valuable experience involving very fast system design, network definition, financial arrangements, tendering, construction, testing and training. It was a good example of excellent cooperation between governments, financial institutions, manufacturers, and also between the North and the South.

The future implications

Technology may have both beneficial and adverse effects. Several observers have cautioned against the loss of privacy, the dehumanisation of individuals, and the exploitation of the information-poor by the information-rich. John Naisbitt, in his book 'Megatrends', published by Warner Books in 1983, identified several trends which have been associated with progress in information and communications technology. He discussed the rapid shift from an industrial society to an information society, such as more decentralisation, moves towards a global economy, restructuring of the work environment and so on. It is not difficult to see that these changes and trends will affect decision makers in all sections of the community. Many other writers have identified general trends in our society. These documented trends, however, have been based mainly on observations made in the industrial countries. Below is a list of some trends in developing countries:

1   There is a trend towards a change and/or restructuring in the way we communicate and in leadership style. The structure of communications in the developing world has been mainly dictated by 'tradition'. The flow of communications has been more 'top-down' rather than 'bottom-up'. The advent of modern communications and information facilities is not only changing that traditional outlook, but also introducing complexities into it, so that it is becoming a 'multidimensional' communications process and flow. This change is calling for a readjustment of our leadership style to become ever more adaptive.

2   There appears to be increasing pressure for the decentralisation of power both in commercial and governmental organisations. Better communications facilities, widespread and easy access to information, as well as an increasing, 'customised' demand for high-quality goods and services, are factors pushing decision makers to decentralise, thus necessitating a restructuring of organisations. We can see this taking place in different forms, such as in the move towards privatisation of telecommunications in Malaysia.

3   The increasing global interconnection is demanding a global outlook by decision makers. A certain inevitability of global interdependence is being felt. In such a situation we must remind ourselves that 'cooperation is the law of life', because through cooperation bigger and more useful goals can be achieved. We must avoid domination and exploitation of one another, because such an approach will break down the common pursuit of the enhancement of our quality of life.

4   The high speed of change will continue to be the pattern of the future. This brings to mind two aspects. One is our adaptability as

decision makers and the other is the importance of human resource development. Education and the conversion of the populations into a technology receptive workforce will certainly be one of the biggest challenges for decision makers.

5 Information and communications technology is our vehicle into the information society. In such a society, information will play a very important role. For those in the developing world, there will be the increasing challenge of what, when and how new technologies are to be utilised.

These then are some points, by no means exhaustive, which depict the challenges that decision makers will face in the developing world in the years to come.

Strategy for development and use of information technology in the developing world

Technology cannot progress or be useful independently of the society in which it operates. It must, therefore, be developed and chosen by the society itself. What about the developing world? As the author has mentioned before, 'cooperation is the law of life'. Thus, one of the basic strategies must be 'international cooperation' which could become a vehicle for a transfer of technology, and a source of financing and managerial know-how. Developing countries must determine their criteria for choosing the technology best suited to development. Developing countries must also give a high priority to human development. Without highly educated and skilled people, no nation can hope to become a serious participant in the world economy. Without a clear strategy, long-term planning and a determination to master successfully needed technologies, the developing world will remain only a 'dreamer of' rather than a possessor of the benefits of information and communications technology.

Conclusions

The author draws the following four conclusions:

1 Progress in information and communications technology has brought unprecedented changes into our world, moving us towards an information society.

2 This progress, unfortunately, has not benefited all of us. While some are enjoying the benefits of the most advanced technology, others, mainly in the developing world, are still waiting for their dreams to come true.

3 The implications of the new technology in the area of information and communications for decision makers include development towards a more global outlook, changes in leadership-style, pressure for the restructuring of organisations, and the need for development of mutually beneficial international cooperation. The environment of rapid change is demanding that decision makers give higher priority to human resource development.

4 Developing nations must design a clear national strategy for technological development and the transfer of technology to suit their own societies; we may not even have the choice not to forge ahead. Information technology will enter our lives and change and influence them without our consent. The goal of decision makers must be to ensure that the new technologies will bring a real enhancement of the quality of life of their people.

Jonathan Parapak

As President Director of INDOSAT, Honorary Lecturer at the University of Indonesia and Chairman of the Board of Commissioners of Graha Informatika Nusantara, Jonathan Parapak is very involved in telecommunications developments within Indonesia and South East Asia. He is an engineer with a degree from the University of Tasmania. He held various positions within Telecoms Australia and ITT, prior to joining INDOSAT in 1981.

PART V

Information Technology and the Individual

There are many aspects to developments in information technologies which have an impact on society and the individual. Some of these are basic issues such as privacy, the dehumanisation of society and the prospects for work out of the home. Most of the issues are complex, and there are a wide range of views on each. The authors deal with two important aspects of information technology's impact on the individual — work and the worldwide transmission of cultural media.

In the case of work, greater unemployment, observed in most economies today, is generally linked with the introduction of information technology in the workplace, thus, fostering negative public opinion about new production methods based on information technology. Future public acceptance of information technology, in general, will depend largely on how decision makers handle this issue. One of the real questions behind the debate is whether, in the long term, man faces a virtually jobless society. Hellmut Schütte addresses this issue and offers an alternative approach to decision makers.

Youichi Ito discusses the worldwide transmission of cultural media, made possible today by improvements in communications technology. While there are certainly possibilities for the mutual enrichment of nations and cultures in the exchange of information and entertainment programmes, there are also possibilities of cultural inundation, where the traditional characteristics of one nation or region are lost or suppressed by another. Assuming the unlimited spread of a few dominant cultures, one might even envisage a world in which most people think, speak, dress and act alike. Cultural traditions would be relegated to museums, dinosaurs in a modern, high-tech world. Such a prospect is frightening to most people; however, if society is to guard against the loss of traditions and cultural differences and, at the same time to profit from the exchange of cultures, decision makers must be aware of the dangers and take steps to foster healthy developments.

Unemployment and the Human Value System

Hellmut Schütte

The impact of information technology on unemployment

A heated debate has developed during the last few years over the impact of information technology on our society. Particularly in Europe, the discussion has focused on the effect of technological change upon employment, and has produced a vast number of studies without leading to any clear-cut and unequivocal conclusions.

Authors and organisations who see the recent progress in the field of information technology as part of a long-term evolution of technical capabilities, consider today's technology-induced unemployment as a limited and temporary phenomenon due to slow adjustment to changing circumstances. Others consider the new information technologies as a revolutionary development forcing upon us major changes in values, processes and institutions. The latter tend to adopt a longer-term view and see the present unemployment as a structural problem.

The debate demonstrates the common difficulties of economic analysis, such as the lack of reliable statistics and experimental verification, and the specific complexities of technological assessment. Not only is the term 'information technology' far from being clearly defined but technology itself is difficult to grasp. It is everywhere and nowhere. The measurement of technological change by calculation of changes in (labour) productivity is equally problematic.

The 'hardest' evidence of the impact of information technology on labour comes from case studies of individual firms and industrial sectors. They describe the direct effects, that is to say, the net changes in jobs at the point of introduction of new technology. The change is — as a rule — negative if the technology is used to improve the production process and increase productivity. Such application of technology leads to capital deepening investment and can mainly be found in countries/sectors with low growth. The direct effect, however, can also be positive, if new technologies lead to new or improved products which create new demands, which in turn can only be satisfied with additional labour. Such application of technology is more characteristic for high-growth environments.

The immediate effects on firms and industrial sectors do not tell of the ripples and waves created by new products and processes on competitors, suppliers and buyers, and thus do not lend themselves to generalisations. There are two indirect effects which need attention. First, increased productivity through new application of technology results in either higher profits for the producers, or, if the benefit is passed on to the consumer, better or cheaper products for the buyer. In any case, the creation of additional wealth will occur. This can (but will not necessarily) lead to additional demand somewhere in the economy, which in turn may (or may not) result in additional jobs.

Second, if the new technologies lead to additional gross investment, this brings additional demand for capital goods and service suppliers which may (but will not necessarily) need additional labour.

These direct and indirect effects are also important in the context of international trade and international competitiveness. Innovative firms which gain an advantage through the application of information technology may compensate for labour displacement with additional jobs created by the success of their export business. Multiplier effects on suppliers and income effects on shareholders may also accrue to the country which introduced new technologies first. Countries resistant to or slow to adopt technological opportunities, on the other hand, will neither benefit from direct or indirect effects, nor experience wealth and job creation in the industry concerned. Protectionism remains to those non-innovative countries an attractive, though in the long-term ineffective, measure to prevent the transfer of jobs to those which lead in the introduction and application of new technology.

The difficulties in coming to any clear conclusions are further aggravated by the fact that information technology, like all technical advances, needs time from the point of innovation to diffusion and application. So far, the time for adjustment to the new technologies has been too short. This applies especially to the institutional and legal frameworks with their enormous impact on labour recruitment and displacement.

Finally, while individuals and firms influence technology, technology itself has an impact on society, which in turn shapes the minds of individuals and firms. This interdependence calls again for a longer-term perspective on change.

Despite all these theoretical and practical problems, and the impossibility of measuring the precise impact of information technology on unemployment, there is at least general agreement that a link does exist. It can be observed in both products and production processes.

In many products large numbers of parts and components are replaced by small numbers of highly integrated electronic components. Additional capabilities are added without great difficulty. In this way the added value shifts from the mainly manual assembly of the final products to the increasingly automated production of components. As a result, less labour is required for better products sold at the same or even lower prices. Computers, television sets and watches are prime examples.

Changes in production processes brought about by the integration of microelectronics and software in existing machines has resulted in automation which represents nothing more than an advanced form of labour-displacing mechanisation. The real breakthrough is achieved by today's programmable automation. This has led to decreasing dedication of machines such as robots or NC-machines to certain processes and products and to increased flexibility. Opportunities now exist to link them up with other information systems within the organisation through Computer-aided Design (CAD), Computer-aided Manufacture (CAM), Computer-integrated Manufacturing (CIM) etc.

Contrary to changes in product technology, changes in production process technology offer, as a rule, the choice between investment in machinery or continuation with labour. It may be for this reason that factory and office automation have played a greater role in the debate about unemployment than the changing nature of products. Interdependencies between product design and production process, and between machines and human beings, in addition to aspects of quality and competitive pressure, have, however, added other dimensions.

Determining factors of unemployment

In a simplified way we may look at unemployment as being the working population minus employees and the self-employed. For comparisons across time or between countries, percentages of the unemployed to the working population are normally used. These comparisons can hide significant variations. The working population — the supply side — is determined by the number of people of working age, that is by demographic factors, and by the labour participation rate, that is the willingness of people of working age to work. The number of employees and to some extent the self-employed — representing the demand side (jobs offered and filled) — is determined mainly by the profit expectations of those who employ them. Profit expectations in turn depend upon demand for the respective products and services and the degree of competitiveness of the specific firms, industrial sectors or countries.

In the US, the working population grew by about 20 million during 1974-84, mainly due to an increasing number of women looking for jobs. Most of those 20 million found jobs, but not all of them, and so, as a result, unemployment grew. A similar development could be observed in Japan. In the larger European countries, however, the opposite happened. The growth of the working population stagnated, but the number of jobs available shrank substantially. Therefore, while the percentage of unemployment rose in all the countries concerned, the reasons for this change differed markedly.

With 31 million unemployed through the Organisation for Economic Cooperation and Development (OECD), 19 million of whom are in OECD Europe, policy makers have made (at least in office statements) the reduction of unemployment a prime objective. This holds especially true for Europe, but applies increasingly to the US and Japan. The eradication of unemployment, however, down to a low level of a frictional residual — an objective seen as achievable in the 1950s and 1960s — has become an unrealistic dream.

There is a clear distinction between those groups who think that governments have to boost demand to create jobs, and those who believe that the supply side rigidities, particularly the quasi fixed price of labour, have to be dismantled in order to allow the market to clear. Trade unionists, opposition parties and disenfranchised economists blame governments for having diverted economic policies away from full employment towards defeating inflation, thereby squeezing demand, reducing output to a recession and, thus, throwing people out of work. Those in charge of such policies respond by blaming unnecessary regulations, the lack of mobility and the increasingly inappropriate skills of those looking for jobs. The truth lies probably somewhere between these two extreme views, and there is growing awareness that any policy, to be at all successful, must attack from both sides.

The experience in recent years is not good. Despite a generally favourable economic climate in most OECD countries, unemployment has not gone down substantially. Additional demand has not created additional jobs because, due to growing productivity, more could be produced by the same or a smaller number of people. The phrase 'jobless growth' has been coined for this phenomenon. Labour markets, such as the American one, which are relatively free of rigidities have accommodated large numbers of job seekers, but mainly in low-skilled or unskilled jobs at very low rates of pay. It is said that many of the newly created jobs in the US pay less than Europeans receive in unemployment benefits. Despite this, even the US under the Reagan administration has experienced its highest unemployment for several decades.

For labour markets to function properly, it would appear that even more than the 'freeing' of the price of labour would be necessary. Removing 'rigidities', such as protection from arbitrary notice, assurance of stable real income, and the system of income transfer and social security, means dismantling the achievements of a century of social reform. Whether markets will function smoothly afterwards remains to be seen, since on both the supply and the demand side a rather heterogeneous group of people and jobs are bunched together representing large numbers of submarkets. What we see already today is an unsatisfied demand for certain skills despite hefty growth in wages, while unskilled workers, in particular, cannot find jobs even at very low rates. Transfers between skilled jobs are equally problematic due to increased specialisation.

Expected changes

Apart from arguments and policies aimed at a better functioning of labour markets, there are three ideas which dominate the public debate at this moment.

The first is based on the belief that people who are displaced in so-called 'sunset' industries will sooner or later find a job in 'sunrise' industries. They consider the decline and growth of industries to be a natural, healthy phenomenon, and any increase in unemployment to be the result of the slow pace of adjustment by the workforce to new opportunities. Unfortunately, evidence does not support this view. Sunrise industries, such as the computer industry, have not provided very many new jobs. In fact, in the American computer industry the total employment in recent years has increased only slowly while the number of production workers in the industry has even decreased. Overall jobs in high technology industries have grown significantly over the last decade, but their growth has been lower than the growth of jobs in the restaurant and hotel business. Due to the small employment base at present and the propensity of high technology industries to use labour-saving equipment, it is not expected that these sectors will provide more than five per cent of total jobs in OECD countries even in the year 1995, despite a continued high growth in output.

The second idea accepts the displacement of labour in industry and compares it with the displacement of labour in the agricultural sector in the past. We are thus moving into the age of an ever-growing service sector, from which, in the future, a fourth sector, a vaguely defined information sector, may evolve. Proponents of this view can point to developments in almost all OECD countries showing a strong growth in jobs in the service sector. However, it is far from being clear whether this development will continue. It is not true that the trend towards the service sector is a one-way street.

As the move into do-it-yourself, the switch from public transport to the private car and from cinema to television proves, a reverse trend, an 'industrialisation' of services is also possible. In fact, McDonald's hamburger outlets can be seen as restaurants and therefore part of the service sector, or as decentralised factories belonging to the manufacturing industry. Also, growth in output and low productivity gains in the past have made additional employment in the sector necessary. With further diffusion of information technology in the Civil Service, retailing, banking and insurance, more work can be done by the same or even fewer people. A continued overall growth of jobs in the service sector, although easily predictable in some subsectors, is thus not assured due to possible contractions in other subsectors.

The third school of thought acknowledges that there will be less and less work and that social systems, such as welfare provisions, cannot be changed. As work becomes increasingly scarce, the issue of its distribution has to be raised. The present attempts to reduce the hours of work per week have to be seen in this light. They are not driven by the need to reduce the burden of overworked labour, but to spread a given workload over more people. Work sharing, extension of education/training before entry into the workforce, re-education/training programmes during active work-life, the lowering of retirement age, and other measures fall to some extent into the same category. It is the underlying assumption which is important: productivity growth is higher than growth in output due to technological change, which itself is mainly driven by progress in information technology. If we consider that the impact of information technology has not yet been fully experienced even in the OECD countries due to rather slow acceptance and diffusion, then we must expect higher productivity growth rates in the foreseeable future.

Going back to our original discussion of supply and demand, we must therefore accept an increasing scarcity of work if we do not succeed in reducing the supply of labour or increasing demand for labour. This means continued, if not growing, unemployment.

The status of work

The implications of such a scenario are far-reaching. The more scarce work becomes, the more the existing fabric of our societies is called into question. People's lives depend on work defined as paid employment. It provides people with direct income and is the basis of transfer income. It structures people's days, years and even lives, in the sense that it is preceded by a period of education and followed by retirement. Finally, it gives people their own identity, their status and self-respect.

It is the last aspect which is the most crucial one. Productivity gained through technological change will create more wealth and enable societies to replace income earned by a working person, at least partly, with unemployment benefits transferred to him when he is not working. We may be able, although this will probably require more effort, to provide people with enough stimuli to undertake meaningful activities in lieu of working. But will we be able to accept people without work as full members of our society? In a society structured around work, what is the purpose of life for somebody without a job?

Protestant ethics, if not all Christianity as well as Confucianism, teach dedication to work and thrifty behaviour as a precondition for deserved well-being. Productive human activity therefore means to work. Usefulness within our societies, as the discussion of payment for housewives for their work at home proves, is defined by receiving wage income. Those who are outside the system are not accepted as full members of our society, they are 'losers' regardless of the reasons for their unemployment.

Those who are affected carry a stigma: the young, the unskilled, the ethnic minorities and the old. Youth unemployment, now particularly high in the UK and Italy, basically deprives the younger generation of the chance to grow up, to become independent. There is growth in drug abuse, alcoholism and crime among young people who may feel they have little to lose.

Those who are unemployed form a class of the deprived. They represent no political force and thus have no political power. There is no solidarity among them, and demonstrations of the unemployed against social injustice, the welfare system or a particular government have hardly been witnessed. The unemployed may, as a floating mass, be prepared to join the demonstrations of others, but on their own they are unlikely to initiate a revolution. They require organisation — and those organisations which exist, trade unions for instance, service those *with* jobs. The options for the individual, too, are limited. He may, if he is lucky, find a short-term or part-time job. Increasingly, however, he will find that those who have work cling to it, while he himself does not succeed in getting it. Long-term unemployment, turning people into unemployables, is gaining ground. Labour unions are beginning to recognise that their achievements benefit only the employed majority, while leaving the unemployed further behind.

Changing the human value system

While policiticans everywhere continue to seek ways to reduce unemployment and economists continue to argue about which policies should be applied to make it happen, there is a growing feeling within the population that unemployment will stay or even grow. A recent opinion poll by the Atlantic Institute across various OECD countries shows that on average more than 50 per cent of the population believe that the increased use of information processing systems (computers, word processors) will worsen unemployment. The view that these systems would help to create jobs was held by only 12 to 25 per cent of those polled outside the US. Among the Americans, however, 50 per cent saw information processing systems as job creators.

So far, according to international organisations such as the OECD and the EEC, the impact of information technology on the total level of employment has not been significant. Their view on the future is less firm except that the semi-skilled and the unskilled — the traditional working class — will be increasingly out of work. Otherwise, there is hope that after sufficient time for adjustment labour markets will somehow find an equilibrium again. The employment organisation as an underlying structure of our life is queried only by very few outside those institutions which follow the developments of labour markets closely. It seems to be difficult to conceive a future without work in its present form.

What will happen if over the next few years work becomes increasingly scarce? Can a scenario for the year 2000 be totally ruled out under which work distribution programmes have been exhausted and unemployment rates have increased in OECD countries to 20, 30 or even 40 per cent? Or, bringing the question down to a more concrete level, are we sure that our children and/or grandchildren will find work in the year 2000 and will not end up on the 'losers' side?

In a historical perspective a paradox becomes apparent. Human beings have worked hard to reduce work only to find that not having enough work destroys the self-respect of the individual and endangers the social structure of our nations.

There is another paradox. As long as unemployment rates stay at levels comparable with those of today, societies will probably not seriously question the underlying assumptions of our value system and see the unemployed as minorities who do not want to work, do not need to work (married women) or do not deserve work (the unskilled, untrained), comforting each other with anecdotes about the difficulties of finding a plumber or employing a gardener.

Only with much larger unemployment rates, perhaps with the unemployed representing the majority of people of working age, may unemployment be seen as a social good and not as a social ill. Only then will work in the classical sense be dethroned, and human activity outside the traditional holding of a paid job be fully recognised as a productive occupation. Then a decoupling of work and income, together with the replacement of unemployment benefits with a minimum guaranteed income for every citizen and a system of positive and negative income tax, may be called for.

Unemployment under such a scenario may all of a sudden not look so much like a threat as an opportunity for people to pursue activities they like, or they feel are important, such as care for the elderly, for the environment etc, while the achievements of information technology, managed by an enthusiastic minority, will continue to create wealth to support the system.

It is easy to call such a scenario unrealistic. It may be so. Redefinition of something which is as central to human life as work, however, is not a question which can be answered with a few words, a few discussions and a few theories. Redefinition of work involves the whole set of values which exist in our societies, which drive our societies, which control our societies. It is connected to religious beliefs as well as to the practicalities of money.

If we are all sure that new technologies will not lead to a scenario of ever-growing unemployment, there is no need to dethrone work. If, however, we cannot be so sure about future developments, and we are already confronted with millions out of work, then decision makers should perhaps begin to think about alternative scenarios.

Further reading

1
Alic J A
'Employment and job creation impacts of high technology — what can be learned from the US example?'
Futures
(Aug 1982)

2
'The electronic future — impact on work and society'
Aslib Proc
Great Britain
(Feb 1982)

3
Blanchard F
'Technology, work and society: some pointers from ILO research'
International Labour Review
vol 123 no 3
Geneva
(May-June 1984)

4
Management and Technology — A Survey of European Chief Executives
1984
Booz-Allen and Hamilton
Paris
(1984)

5
Europe 1995. Mutations Technologiques et Enjeux Sociaux
Rapport FAST
Futuribles
Commission of the European Communities
(1983)

6
Economie Européenne

no 25
Commission of the European Communities
(Sep 1985)

7
Dahrendorf Ralf von
'Für jeden bürger ein garantiertes Einkommen'
Die Zeit
(17 Jan 1986)

8
Freeman C and Soete L
Information Technology and Employment: An Assessment
University of Sussex
(Apr 1985)

9
Friedrichs G and Schaff A
Auf Gedeih und Verderb — Mikroelektronik und Gesellschaft
Europaverlag Vienna
(1982)

10
Handy C B
The Future of Work — A Guide to a Changing Society
Basil Blackwell Inc Oxford
(1984)

11
Influence of Microelectronics on Employment
Japan Ministry of Labour
(Apr 1984)

12
Leontief W and Duchin F
The Impacts of Automation on Employment 1963-2000
New York Univ
(Apr 1984)

13
Employment Outlook
OECD Paris
(1984 and 1986)

14
Microelectronics, Robotics and Jobs
ICCP rep
no 7
OECD
(1982)

15
Information Activities, Electronics and Telecommunications Technologies: Impacts on Employment, Growth and Trade
OECD
(1984)

16
Rumberger R W and Levin H M
'Forecasting the impact of new technologies on the future job market'
Technological Forecasting and Social Change
no 27
(1985)

17
Wilson R and Whitley J
'Quantifying the employment effects of microelectronics'
Futures
vol 14 no 6
(Dec 1982)

18
Donges J B
'Chronic unemployment in Western Europe forever?'
The World Economy
(Dec 1985)

Hellmut Schütte

Joining INSEAD's Euro-Asia Centre in 1981, Professor Schütte is
responsible for teaching and research in the areas of international trade,
international marketing and international business, with a specialisation
in Asian affairs. He has a strong orientation towards technological issues.
In the past, Professor Schütte has worked as the Regional Manager in the
Philippines for the German Development Company — a German gov-
ernment-owned, investment bank — and as an executive for Unilever, a
large Dutch/British multinational, both in Europe and Asia.

Global Communication and Cultural Identity: An East Asian Perspective

Youichi Ito

There is no human culture on this earth which has never learned anything from another. Learning from other cultures is a natural phenomenon and there is nothing wrong with it. However, when foreign influence is overwhelming, beyond the control of the receiving country, or one way for a long period of time, psychologically delicate problems emerge.

All people in the world want to be equal, not only in principle, but also in practice. If Nation A always influences Nation B and Nation B never influences Nation A for an extended period of time, people in Nation B will begin to feel that their culture is inferior; their cultural identity may be endangered. In such circumstances, people in Nation B may suffer from an inferiority complex and begin to resent Nation A. In the extreme case, Nation B loses cultural integrity, imagination, creativity and energy and is eventually led to a complete cultural and social collapse. Unfortunately, a few examples of this extreme case exist.

On the other hand, if Nation A and Nation B influence each other and learn from each other, the cultures of the two nations will both be enriched and the welfare of both nations will be enhanced. In the past, new leaps in human cultures and civilisations have often been brought about by the blending and synthesising of different cultural elements. Such cultural leaps benefit the people of the world and there exist many examples of this kind of progress.

The extremely rapid development of modern communication technologies has accelerated the speed of culture transmission among different nations. If the present world situation follows the second scenario, that is increase of mutual influence, there is no need for concern. However, many experts, particularly those in Third World countries, are afraid that the world might be following the first scenario, that is cultural domination on one hand, and cultural subordination and collapse on the other. The following, are the author's views on the validity and limitations of this latter theory, considering the situation in East Asia where there are many countries with long cultural traditions and rapidly developing economies.

The cultural imperialism theory as seen by the Japanese

The cultural imperialism theory assumes that information flows from the information-rich areas, such as the West or the North, to the information-poor areas, such as the non-West or the South; it assumes that these flows are changing the cultures or even endangering the cultural identities of non-Western or Southern nations. In this popular theory, Japan is in a unique position. Japan belongs to the information-rich North but also to the non-West which has received a massive flow of information from the West. Longitudinal trends of international information flow coming into and going out of Japan indicate that, roughly speaking, Japan was an information-poor, non-Western country until the late 1960s, but has become an information-rich, Northern country since the early 1970s. At present, Japan is one of the major information exporting countries and the amount of information that Japan imports from other countries is relatively small.

Using television as an indicator of information flows, it can be noted that Japan exports twice as many television programmes as it imports from other countries. Japan exports three times more television programmes to Europe than it imports from Europe. The television programme trade between the US and Japan is almost balanced. The trade of long films between Japan and the rest of the world is almost balanced. The percentage of foreign television programmes shown in Japan is the second lowest in the world after the US. The percentage is even lower during 'prime time' viewing hours. Most foreign programmes are broadcast either late at night or during the daytime. The American drama series 'Dallas', an uncontested success in many countries, was cancelled in Japan after six months because the average rating never went up to more than five per cent. In addition *Readers Digest Japan* went bankrupt after many years of deficit operation.

If we compare the strength of Japan's sense of cultural identity in the 1960s with that of the 1980s, it appears that the Japanese in the 1980s have a stronger sense of cultural identity than in the 1960s. The most important reason for the heavy importation of foreign media products before 1970 was the weak competitiveness of the Japanese mass media products. Another important reason could have been the weak sense of cultural identity among the Japanese people before 1970. Japan imported many foreign mass media products when the nation's sense of cultural identity was weak. Foreign media products steadily disappeared from the Japanese market as the sense of identity became stronger. It seems, therefore, that weak cultural identity could be a *cause* of the importation of foreign media products rather than a result of it. At the same time, what cannot be denied is the possibility that the excessive importation of foreign media products weakens the cultural identity of the people in the importing country. Under certain conditions, there may be such effects.

If, however, it is the case that excessive importation of foreign media weakens cultural identity then why do the modern Japanese have a strong sense of cultural identity despite Japan often being regarded as one of the most 'Westernised' countries in the non-Western world? Why did Japan's sense of cultural identity strengthen after 1970? Does economic and technological progress automatically strengthen a people's sense of cultural identity? These issues are discussed from a theoretical viewpoint in the next section.

Theoretical considerations on cultural identity in non-Western countries

In discussions of the cultural imperialism theory, the Japanese case has often been ignored by some as an embarrassing exception. Others maintain that Japan has become so Westernised that it is already 'a kind of Western country'. These two approaches are both fundamentally incorrect. First, present-day Japan is too important to neglect as an embarrassing exception. Also, as discussed later in this paper, what has happened in Japan is very likely to happen in the near future in other rapidly developing East Asian countries and regions, such as South Korea, Hong Kong, Taiwan, Singapore and Malaysia. Second, those who regard Japan as 'a kind of "Western country" fail to distinguish the difference between "modernisation" and "Westernisation"'.

Modernisation refers to the advancement of a culture or civilisation in the competitive sector. The competitive sector includes those aspects of a civilisation which people can easily compare, determining which is superior or inferior. In such areas, most nations in the world attempt to increase their ranking with regard to one another for the sake of national pride. Military strength is a classic item in this sector. Competition for military strength between different human groups has existed since the beginning of human culture and civilisation. Before the industrial revolution, the numbers of soldiers and advanced weaponry were the most important factors determining military strength. After the industrial revolution, industrial strength and economic scale also became crucial factors for a strong military. As a result, industrial strength and economic scale joined the competitive sector of human culture and civilisation. Most recently, technology has been recognised to be a crucial factor for a strong military and a strong economy. In the competitive sector of human culture and civilisation, there is no Westernisation or Easternisation. What looks like Westernisation or Easternisation is usually nothing but advancement which permits nations to catch up with superior or more developed nations in the competitive sectors.

There are many aspects of human culture and civilisation in which competition is not involved. Language, religion, ideology, value systems, customs, way of life, way of thinking, music, fine arts and stage arts are some examples. These belong to the non-competitive sector of a culture or civilisation. If we are to judge fairly the level of foreign cultural influence, then concepts such as Westernisation, Americanisation, Japanisation, etc, should be limited to this non-competitive sector of culture. For instance, if the Japanese nation accepts Christianity as a result of the Western influence, it is Westernisation. However, Japan's economic or technological development or military build-up *per se* is not Westernisation but simply an attempt to increase its ranking with regard to its international competitors.

It is true that a change in the competitive sector of culture can and does affect the non-competitive sector and vice versa. For example, Japan's economic development has affected Japanese traditional values, customs, ways of living and thinking. On the other hand, Japan's traditional values, customs, ways of living and thinking have had an effect upon Japan's economic development.

Often, people tend to justify success in the competitive sector by traits in the non-competitive sector. For example, many Westerners have believed that Christianity, individualism, and Western rationalism are the prerequisites for industrial success. This is not necessarily the case. Japan succeeded in industrialisation without adopting any of these Western prerequisites. (As for the meaning of rationalism, more detailed discussions are necessary.) This kind of justification has led to confusion between the concepts of modernisation (in the competitive sector) and Westernisation (in the non-competitive sector).

A historical review

The history of war and the military is as old as that of human culture and civilisation. The military existed long before the establishment of sophisticated human culture and civilisation. Most people in the world were aware of the competitive nature of the military, and all cultural items were forced into harmony with the existence and activities of the military. Manufacturing industries, economic organisations and systems, and science and technology *did* exist in ancient and medieval East and South Asia and the Arab World. Medieval Europe learned much from manufacturing techniques and science and technology imported from the Orient. Before the industrial revolution, however, the importance of industrial and economic strength and technology was not fully understood, even by national leaders. It was modern Europe, and later the US, which drastically developed manufacturing industries, economies and technologies to the extent that the nations without them were likely to be colonised and enslaved. Since the 19th century, industrial and economic strength and technology have come to have similar international implications as the military had in the ancient and medieval worlds.

In the mass society of the 20th century, the importance of economic and technological developments comes not only from their military implications. The masses demand a higher quality of life. Before World War Two, national leaders tried to meet such demands by invading or colonising weaker nations and exploiting their wealth and labour. After World War Two, however, all the nations in the world agreed that such actions were unethical and should be banned. In the present day world, economic and technological development is the only way to meet the widespread demand for a higher quality of life.

Industrialisation and technological development required various resources such as a well-organised bureaucracy, diligent workers, entrepreneurship, a high level of education, etc. Traditional societies, however, could not provide these resources all at once. Moreover, some traditional values and customs (in the non-competitive sector) obstructed the provision of these resources. Such obstacles and the resulting frictions in society existed even in Europe where the industrial and scientific revolutions were initiated. Ogburn *(ITO1)* called such phenomena 'cultural lag' between the industrial and non-industrial sectors. In the Western world, however, such frictions were resolved or at least eased as a result of compromise or adaptation on the part of the non-competitive sector. Eventually, the Western world reached the stage where supremacy in the competitive sector could be justified by legacies from the non-competitive sector.

In non-Western countries where the industrial revolution was imported from outside, the adjustment was far more difficult because there was comparatively little time to make adjustments which, in the West, had taken over a century. The adaptations appeared so difficult to make and time was so limited that national leaders in underdeveloped countries, particularly those who were educated in the West, were frequently tempted to import the Western model as a block. This policy often included the change of religion or written and/or spoken languages. Even in Japan and China, there were recommendations in the past to abandon Chinese ideograms and Japanese characters and replace them with Roman letters to facilitate modernisation.

Drastic cultural reform, however, is dangerous, particularly in those countries with long histories of civilisation. The majority of the population has a strong attachment to the traditional way of life and doing things, and many people's lives are dependent on old customs and economic systems. Emotional reactions and practical interests combine, and thus a strong reactionary movement against cultural reform is born and spreads.

While struggling to overcome the 'cultural lag' between the competitive and non-competitive sectors, many non-Western countries were invaded and colonised by major Western powers which succeeded in, at least, controlling if not resolving the 'lag' in an exceptionally short period of time. In the end, colonisation confused the adjustment process in the colonised countries and delayed the process even further. Many developing countries are still struggling with a gap between the competitive and non-competitive sectors. Some feel that there are certain countries which will never catch up in the competitive sector, because their basic values and ways of life in the non-competitive sector are not at all harmonious with industrialisation or technological development.

In such cases, there is a large problem of cultural identity. The cultural identity issue relates to a nation's sense of continuity. When people cannot relate what they are doing or plan to do with what they have been doing in the past, they have an identity problem. The Japanese have experienced this identity problem twice in their history, in the late 19th century and soon after World War Two. Before World War Two, Japan combined medieval militaristic tradition with modern military strength, a modern economy and new technology to develop and support military efforts. Thus, the Japanese before World War Two managed to maintain continuity.

This sense of continuity was shattered by defeat in World War Two. The Japanese lost confidence and suffered from an identity crisis and an inferiority complex. This state continued until the middle of the 1960s when the Japanese economy reached the level of advanced industrialised countries. At the end of the 1960s, a new search for identity began in Japan, and many books and articles were written on this subject. This phenomenon was called the *nihonjin ron* (studies of Japanese people and culture) boom. It was a very long and thorough period of intellectual activity involving journalists, social critics, academics, political leaders, leftists, conservatives and foreign Japanologists. One of the functions of this intellectual boom was to relate Japan's industrial and technological success to its traditional cultural legacies.

Today, Japan's industrial and technological success is explained in Japan by Confucian work ethics, with the emphasis on group harmony and consensus, inter-group (rather than inter-individual) competition, and Confucian views on education and social order, etc. Japanese perfectionistic pursuit of quality in industrial products is related to the ethics of traditional craftsmanship. A Korean scholar published a bestseller book in Japanese in which he characterised the Japanese technology as the 'technology of miniaturisation' and related modern Japanese electronic products to the philosophy behind the Japanese garden, *bonsai*, *hakoniwa* (miniature landscape) and other traditional fine arts *(ITO2)*. The so-called Japanese management is based on traditional Japanese views on human relations, groups, and social organisations. The Japanese management style has also had a strong impact on management styles in other nations. The modern Japanese way of life, consisting of Video Cassette Recorders (VCRs), home computers and compact disks, is often associated with the Japanese garden and *bonsai*. Today, many Japanese believe that the Japanese way of life is influencing the life-styles of other nations.

Some of these theories may sound too ethnocentric and may not be acceptable to people outside Japan or East Asia. However, considering the existence of many ethnocentric theories in the West, the birth of such theories should be regarded as a natural phenomenon. Besides, these justifications are probably more acceptable to other countries than would be Japanese regression to the samurai traditions. Thus, at least at the Japanese popular level, it seems that modern Japan and traditional Japan are quite successfully bridged. Japan has succeeded not only in the competitive sector, but also in harmonising or bridging the competitive and non-competitive (or traditional) sectors of its culture.

Japan's success indicates that the futures of East Asian, particularly North East Asian, countries are very promising because the non-competitive elements of their cultures are very similar to those of Japan. Without

SIIT—K

imperialistic invasion and colonialisation by Western powers and Japan, at least China and Korea could have been as successful as Japan in modernisation. As for Mainland China and North Korea, at present, there exist some unpredictable elements because of their adoption of the Communist system. The futures of South Korea, Hong Kong, Taiwan and Singapore are the most promising because they share with Japan the Confucian values and ethics. South East Asian countries do not share the Confucian traditions with Japan; however, their customs and values regarding group and human relations are much more similar to those of Japan than those of the West or South and West Asia, where individualism is more prevalent. East Asian countries appear to have an advantage over developing countries in other parts of the world because the methodology behind bridging the gap between the competitive and the non-competitive sectors has already been tried and proven by the Japanese. This can be regarded as one of the explanations for the 'Look East' policy in Malaysia and the 'Learn from Japan' campaign in Singapore. As a result, it can be concluded that the problem of cultural identity and continuity is less serious in East Asia than in other underdeveloped regions. This will have a desirable effect on economic development as well as on the pattern of international information flow.

Empirical findings regarding cultural flows in East Asia

MASS CULTURE

Television programmes
The share of imported television programmes in Japan used to be quite large in the late 1950s and early 1960s. The peak was the early 1960s. At that time, most popular American programmes were imported and televised in Japan. However, imported programmes gradually lost popularity and were replaced by Japanese programmes over the following 10 years. When Varis (ITO3) investigated the percentages of foreign programmes in major television stations in 53 countries in 1971, the percentage of foreign programmes was one per cent on Nippon Hoso Kyokai (NHK) Educational, four per cent on NHK General, and 10 per cent on the average commercial networks. The percentage of imported television programmes in Japan was the second lowest in the world after the US.

In 1980, a study done by Sugiyama (ITO4) investigated the number of foreign television programmes on seven Japanese television stations. Foreign programmes accounted for 2.3 per cent of the titles and 4.9 per cent of the actual time on these seven stations. The difference between titles and time is due to the fact that most foreign programmes are movies which last an hour and a half or two hours. Among all the imported programmes, 78.1 per cent came from North America, 19.3 per cent from Western Europe, 1.3 per cent from Eastern Europe, 1.0 per cent from Asia, and 0.3 per cent from Oceania.

The same study shows that Japan exported 4585 hours of television programmes to 58 countries in 1980. From the time of Varis' investigation in 1971, Japan's export of television programmes had doubled, while Japan's import remained almost the same. The largest buyers of Japanese exports were the US (1357 hours), followed by Italy (767 hours), Hong Kong (391 hours), South Korea (284 hours) and Taiwan (185 hours).

As a percentage of the total amount of hours of television programmes traded in 1981, imports occupied 33.7 per cent and exports 66.3 per cent. In other words, Japan exported twice as many television programmes as it imported. Table 1 shows the Japanese export/import balance of television programmes by region.

Table 1: Export/import balance of television programmes by region

	Imports (hours)	Exports (hours)
Asia	24	1182
Oceania	3	41
Middle East	2	120
Africa	3	41
Western Europe	429	1121
Eastern Europe	31	33
North America	1820	1407
South America	0	444

Source: Sugiyama (ITO4), 1982

This table shows that the trade of television programmes between the US and Japan is almost balanced and that Japan exports to Western Europe three times more than it imports from Western Europe. This fact is often ignored or underestimated in discussions regarding the international flow of information between Western and non-Western countries. The Japanese experience suggests that it is possible for non-Western countries to improve their balance of international information flows.

Television programmes intrude into homes and dominate ordinary citizens' 'information environment'. Therefore, many people fear that imported television programmes will drastically change the traditional way of life and endanger the cultural identity of the nation. If dominance of foreign programmes continues for more than 100 years, there may be such a danger. The Japanese experience indicates, however, that such a drastic change in cultural identity does not occur within 10 or 20 years even if television networks carry many foreign programmes. What actually happened in Japan is that as television production ability developed, domestic programmes began to top foreign shows in terms of ratings and foreign programmes gradually disappeared from Japanese networks without any government intervention.

Table 2 compares average ratings of imported and domestic programmes. As shown in this table, the ratings of imported programmes, particularly those of entertainment programmes, are much lower than those of Japanese programmes. Therefore, imported programmes seldom appear during prime time in Japan. For example, a researcher checked the programmes of seven television channels available in Tokyo from the 1 to the 30 April 1975, and counted how many times imported programmes appeared during prime time (seven to ten in the evening). They appeared only six times. In other words, imported programmes are televised in Japan late at night or during the daytime for special interest groups rather than for the general public.

Table 2: Comparison of imported and domestic programme ratings

	Imported programmes (%)	Japanese programmes (%)
Drama	5.6	8.8
Comedy	6.4	8.9
Light entertainment	1.1	6.9
Competition	2.9	8.6
Serious performance	1.3	1.1
Information elaboration	5.6	4.9
News	—	0.2
Academic education	—	1.4
Education time slot	9.2	1.4
Enrichment	—	3.7
Value projection	-	3.5
Total	5.1	6.2

Source: Sugiyama (ITO4), 1982

As mentioned before, the share of imported television programmes used to be quite large, but these programmes gradually lost popularity and were replaced by Japanese programmes. The order of disappearance of foreign programmes is interesting. The more culturally bound, the earlier they disappeared. For example, home comedies, variety shows, and drama series made in foreign countries disappeared from Japanese television by 1970. The foreign television programmes that have survived since 1970 are detective stories, movies featuring war, horror, gangsters (such as The Godfather), love and sex. In other words, violence, horror and sex are truly international and cross-cultural entertainment.

In 1981, a major Japanese commercial network decided to introduce the American drama series, 'Dallas', on prime time because its ratings were extremely high, not only in the US but also in Europe and Australia. The company made a large investment in a promotion campaign. The programme was televised once every week from nine to ten in the evening which is an exceptionally favourable time band for a foreign programme. However, the ratings were so low that the series was cancelled after six months. The average rating of 24 episodes televised during the six months was only 4.8 per cent. As this event symbolises, it is very risky for Japanese networks to place foreign programmes on prime time. When asked why they do not like foreign programmes, some people, particularly those in rural areas, replied that they could not remember the European names in the dramas. Others claimed that they could not differentiate the faces of characters, saying, 'Faces of Westerners all look alike'.

What happened in Japanese television is now happening in some newly industrialised countries in Asia. In Singapore and Malaysia, for example, it was reported that the most popular programme category in terms of ratings is domestic programmes, the second is Chinese (Hong Kong and Taiwan) and Japanese programmes, and lastly is the American and European programme category which is, on average, the least popular.

Films and magazines

As a percentage of the total amount of international trade in long films, imports occupied 53.7 per cent and exports 46.3 per cent in Japan in 1977. This means that the trade of long films was almost balanced. One of the characteristics of Japan's film trade was that 93 per cent of the long films Japan imported came from North America and Europe, and only 5.6 per cent came from Asia. On the other hand, 52.9 per cent of Japanese films were exported to Asia and only 23.9 per cent went to North America and Europe. These figures indicate that Japanese long films are less competitive than its television programmes in the international market. A major reason seems to be that in the world's television programme market, the US and Japan are far stronger than other countries, but when it comes to feature length films there are several other European and Asian countries which produce internationally competitive products.

Table 3: The world market shares of exported films

Order	Country	Number	Percentage
	TOTAL	19 230	100
1	US	6645	35
2	Italy	2691	14
3	UK	1713	9
4	France	1558	8
5	India	929	5
6	FRG (West Germany)	680	4
7	USSR	410	2
8	Hong Kong	400	2
9	Turkey	215	1
10	Egypt	210	1
11	Japan	187	1
12	Greece	183	1
13	Spain	107	
14	Sweden	83	
15	Czechoslovakia	60	
16	GDR (East Germany)	59	
17	Poland	55	
18	Denmark	51	
19	Mexico	44	
20	Iran	40	
21	Hungary	38	
22	Yugoslavia	36	
23	Romania	32	
24	Argentina	19	
25	Korea (North)	13	

Source: UNESCO (ITO5), 1975

UNESCO collects data on the import and export of long films from more than 100 countries in the world and publishes the results in its Statistical Yearbook every year. Table 3 shows the market shares of major film exporting countries. As seen from this table, some developing countries which are relatively developed in the region to which they belong and which have rich cultural heritages, such as India, Egypt, Turkey and Hong Kong, occupy relatively large shares of the world's film export market. Today, these countries produce more films than most advanced industrialised countries, and the shares of these countries in the film export market are steadily increasing. A major reason for this trend is that in advanced industrialised countries the film industry is declining due to competition with television, but in some large developing countries, the diffusion rate of television is still so low that movies play an important role as a mass medium entertainment. The domination of the world's film market by North America and Western Europe is apparently coming to an end.

In the Japanese domestic market, the trend in the long film market followed a similar pattern to that of the television market. In the 1950s and 1960s when the Japanese film industry was still feeble, many foreign films were imported. As the Japanese film industry became more competitive, the number of imported films decreased. Most of the foreign films that attracted a large audience were those featuring violence, horror and sex, rather than artistic films which require some background knowledge about the cultures and histories of foreign countries.

Today, Japan exports more books and magazines than it imports. The export-import ratio of books and magazines in Japan in 1977 was 61.5 per cent versus 38.5 per cent. Thirty-two per cent of Japanese books and magazines were exported to Oceania, 25.5 per cent to Asia, 23.5 per cent to North America, 12 per cent to Europe, and 6.6 per cent to other regions. On the other hand, of all imported books and magazines, 44.4 per cent came from North America, 35.2 per cent from Europe, 19.7 per cent from Asia and 0.7 per cent from the rest of the world including Oceania.

Japanese editions of *Playboy* and *Penthouse* are successful whereas *Readers Digest Japan* went bankrupt in 1985 after many years of deficit operation. The reason seems obvious. You need some background knowledge about American society, economy and culture to enjoy reading *Readers Digest*, but one does not need this kind of background to enjoy reading *Playboy* or *Penthouse*. It is very likely that what happened in the Japanese magazine market will also happen in markets in other non-Western countries.

HIGH QUALITY CULTURE

A large portion of high quality culture is exported in the form of hardback books and translations. Unfortunately, there are no statistics regarding the trade of hardback books. However, the flows of translations into and from the Japanese language indicate that Japan is very weak in this area. These figures indicate that Japan's import of high quality culture, chiefly from the West, still overwhelmingly exceeds its exports in this area. In 1979, 2156 books in 14 major foreign languages were translated into Japanese, whereas only 164 titles were translated from Japanese into foreign languages. Out of 2156 titles, 1487 were from English. If we add French (240) and German (230), 91 per cent of translations were from these three languages *(ITO5)*.

Considering the Japanese strength in the world's mass media market, this weakness in translations is interesting and needs some analysis. Generally speaking, most books translated from one language to another belong to high quality culture, rather than mass culture, and science and technology. If we can accept this assumption, three explanations are conceivable for Japan's weakness in translations.

First, although Japan has succeeded in internationalising its popular culture, it has not yet succeeded in internationalising its traditional high quality culture. Second, Japan is still underdeveloped in the basic sciences, particularly social sciences; therefore, many books on social sciences still have to be translated from Western languages. The third explanation is that the largest target for Japanese cultural products, the Asian masses, have not yet reached the stage of enjoying foreign high quality culture. Although the first two reasons cannot be ignored, the third reason seems to be the most important, considering the fact that the Asian market is the largest market for Japanese cultural products. For example, in the UNESCO figures, data on translations in Chinese, a language spoken by more than one billion people, is not available. When people in neighbouring Asian countries reach the stage where they can enjoy translated foreign books, translation of Japanese books into foreign languages will become far more common than at present.

Conclusion

Television programmes, long films, music tapes, records and other mass culture products are produced and sold on the international market just like any other manufactured goods. First of all, in order to produce internationally competitive mass culture products, a country's domestic market has to be sufficiently large. In order to export these products, a country has to have international sales networks and some know-how about trade, advertising and marketing. For these reasons, Japan is quite strong in this area, particularly in Asian markets.

In the countries where domestic products are available, cultural differences work as an effective barrier against imported products. The more culturally bound the content of the imported goods, the more important this element becomes. Therefore, between culturally different countries, excessive influence of foreign cultures will not be a serious problem. However, between culturally similar countries, such as between the US and Canada, the US and Europe, Japan and Korea, and Japan and Taiwan, this can be a serious problem. After all, in the area of mass culture products, industrial strength is a spear and cultural identity is a shield.

A large portion of high quality culture is exported in the form of books and translations. Here also, cultural differences work as a barrier against imports, and it is very difficult for any country to export its traditional or modern high quality culture to other countries. Fortunately, worldwide interest in Japanese traditional and modern high quality culture has grown in recent years. This phenomenon seems to be due to the increase in Japan's economic and political influence. It also explains why Western countries have had such remarkable success exporting their high quality culture over the past two centuries.

Science and technology are universal in nature. Cultural differences virtually do not apply to these sectors. Thus cultural difference does not function as a barrier against the inflow of science and technology. Information regarding science and technology simply flows from upper places to lower places.

At present, the Japanese case is still an embarrassing exception for the cultural imperialism theory. However, what has already happened between the West and Japan is likely to happen between the West and the whole of East Asia in the near future for the following two reasons. First, economies in the East Asian region are generally more developed than in other underdeveloped parts of the world. Therefore, the domestic media infrastructure is in the process of being strengthened. Secondly, the non-competitive sector of East Asian culture seems to be more harmonious with economic and technological development than that of some other non-Western regions. Theories to bridge the gap between economic and technological advancement and East Asian cultural traditions are abundant and have been applied in the case of Japan. Using the Japanese experience as a model, it will be easier for people in East Asia to bridge the gap between the competitive and non-competitive sectors. As a result, East Asia will be able to develop economically and technologically while maintaining a strong sense of cultural identity; cultural difference will come to function as an effective barrier against the excessive import of foreign media products.

On the other hand, the cultural imperialism theory will continue to have validity between countries with similar cultural backgrounds, such as between the US and Canada, the US and Europe, Europe and Australia, Japan and South Korea, Japan and Taiwan, and so forth.

Another point to be emphasised is the importance of maintaining a geographical balance. Excessive importation of information and cultural products is not a serious problem if they are imported from geographically and culturally diverse areas. The problem has become serious because most countries import from only a handful of advanced industrialised countries which have strong marketing capabilities. If information and cultural product exchange systems are developed and each country exchanges its products with a variety of countries, import of information and cultural products will benefit every nation in the world.

The information and discussions provided in this paper may be used for policies to increase export and decrease import of information and cultural products. Since excessive import of foreign culture is a serious problem for most countries in the world, such an approach is understandable. However, the educational value of imported information and cultural products should not be underestimated. Generally speaking, the import of information and cultural products from foreign countries is desirable unless cultural identity is endangered by those imports; it adds something new to the national culture and enriches it. There is no culture in the world which has not, over time, learned and borrowed from another culture. All the great cultures and civilisations in the past were created by the borrowing and blending of many and varied foreign cultures.

References

ITO1
Ogburn W F
Social Change: With Respect to Culture and Original Nature
Huebsch New York
(1922)

ITO2
Lee O-Y
'Chijimi' Shikou no Nihonjin)'Contraction'-oriented Japanese)
Gakusei-sha Tokyo
(1982)

ITO3
Varis T
International Inventory of Television Programme Structure and the Flow of TV Programmes Between Nations
Institute of Journalism and Mass Communication
University of Tampere Tampere Finland
(1973)

ITO4
Sugiyama M
'Television programme imports' (Chapter II)
'Television programme exports' (Chapter III)

'Television programme exports vs imports' (Chapter IV)
In Television Programme Imports and Exports
pp 7-35
NHK Public Opinion Research Institute Tokyo
(1982)

ITO5
UNESCO
Statistical Yearbook (Japanese edition)
Hara Shobo Tokyo
(1975, 1984)

Further reading

1
Ito Y and Kochevar J J
'Factors accounting for the flow of international communication'
Keio Communication Review
vol 4 pp 13-37
(1983)

2
Ito Y and Kochevar J J
'Terebi Bangumino Kokusaikan no Nagare no Kitei Youin ni Kansuru
Kenkyuu' (A study on the factors determining the international flow of
television programmes)
In Kenkyuu Hokoku: Hoso ni Kansuru Horitsu, Keizai, Shakai Bunkateki
Kenkyuu Chousa
pp 98-107
Hoso Bunka Foundation Tokyo
(1984)

3
Katz E and Wedell G
Broadcasting in the Third World
Harvard University Press Cambridge MA
(1977)

4
Kawatake, K (ed)
'Terebi no Naka no Gaikoku Bunka' (Foreign cultures in television)
Nihon Hoso Shuppan Kyokai Tokyo
(1983)

V: IT and the Individual

5
Lee C-C
Media Imperialism Reconsidered
London, Beverely Hills
(1980)

6
Lyle J, Ogawa D and Thomas J D
'Japanese programs in the United States: a widening window on another culture'
Keio Gijuku Daigaku Shimbun Kenkyuujo Nempo
vol 27
no 1-18
(1986)

7
McCombs M E
'Assessing the impact of international communication'
In New Perspectives in International Communication
J Richstad (ed)
pp 71-84
East-West Center
Honolulu HI
(1977)

8
Ministry of Posts and Telecommunications
Tsuushin ni Kansuru Genjou Houkoku (Tsuushin Hakusho) (White Paper on Communications)
Seifu Kankoh Batsu Tokyo
(1978)

9
Mowalana H
Global Information and World Communication
Longman New York
(1985)

10
Schiller H I
'Freedom from the "free flow"'
J of Communication
vol 24 no 1 pp 110-117
(1974)

11
Schiller H I
Communication and Cultural Domination
International Arts and Sciences Press White Plains NY
(1976)

Youichi Ito

Professor Ito is presently the Vice-director of the Institute for Communications Research at Keio University in Tokyo. He has obtained degrees from the School of Public Communication at Boston University, from Keio University and from the Fletcher School of Law and Diplomacy at Tufts University. He is a well-recognised writer, with many English language publications, including Telecommunications Regulation and Deregulation in Industrial Democracies (Longman Communication Books, 1986), and Alternative Mass Communication Systems: The Third World, China and Japan (Hillsdale, New Jersey: Lawrence Erlbaum, forthcoming).

PART VI

Information Technology and the New Economic Paradigm

Present developments in information technologies could be just another group of technical innovations which will soon settle into an industrial sector. As such, they will remain a neatly defined compartment of the economy; computers, silicon chips, communication services and information will be bought and sold just like plastics and polyester.

Yet, some of the innovations in information technology are introducing new ways of functioning and thinking in our personal as well as professional lives. They deal with the sector of human life which has been crucial to man's development through the ages and which constantly allows us to adapt and advance further — that of knowledge. Gathering, sorting and analysing information are basic functions of all intelligent beings.

Chris Freeman believes that information technology is more than just another new technology or industry, and, in his paper, he presents his views and provides an integrated analysis of information technology's impact on society and the economy.

Information Technology and the New Economic Paradigm

Chris Freeman

This paper addresses information technology's present and potential impact on industrialised economies and societies. To accomplish this, the paper examines technical innovations, proposing a format for their classification, and then argues that the combination of radical innovations in computers and telecommunications constitutes a change of 'techno-economic' paradigm. Such a change of paradigm affects all industries and services and brings with it the need for many organisational, managerial and social changes so that the institutional and social framework is well adapted to the potential of the new technologies.

The second part of the presentation discusses the problems of adaptation and structural change and the uneven pattern of productivity growth between industries and countries. It concludes that this uneven pattern will confront decision makers at the enterprise level, national level and international level, with the need to develop some new institutions.

Taxonomy of technical change and diffusion of new technologies

In his book, *Explaining Technical Change* (FRE1), Elster describes two main approaches to technical change:

> 'First, technical change may be conceived of as a rational goal-directed activity, as the choice of the best innovation among a set of feasible changes. Secondly, technical change may be seen as the cumulative addition of small and largely random modifications of the production process. Any serious student of technology will agree that technical change exhibits both these aspects, but there are strong differences in emphasis between the contending explanations.'

SIIT L

159

There is a third approach to technical change which, while recognising that both the other approaches have a domain of validity, allows also for major impulses to technical change; these arise neither exclusively from rational choice nor yet from cumulative small modifications, but from new combinations of radical innovations linking major advances in science and technology with organisational and social innovations. These 'new technological systems' or paradigms can offer such great technical and economic advantages in a wide range of industries and services that their adoption becomes a necessity in any economy exposed to competitive economic, social, political and military pressures. The worldwide diffusion of such new techno-economic paradigms dominates the process of technical change for several decades and powerfully influences economic and social developments even though it does not uniquely determine them. The impulse to develop such new paradigms itself arises from the persistent competitive pressures to sustain profitability and productivity, and from perceived limits to growth of an established paradigm.

Consideration of the empirical research on technical change and innovation, as well as the Schumpeterian and the 'demand-pull' literature, suggests the need for a taxonomy of innovation which distinguishes between incremental innovation, radical innovation, new technological systems and new technological paradigms. In our own work on technical change in the post-war UK economy we *(FRE2* and *FRE3)* found that in all sectors, despite the great variety of specific incremental and radical innovations in almost every industry, there was evidence of a change of 'paradigm' from the capital intensive, energy intensive, inflexible, mass and flow production technology of the 1950s and 1960s, to an information intensive, flexible, computerised technology in the 1970s and 1980s. Such pervasive shifts in technology affecting many or all branches of the economy, as well as other combinations of technical and organisational innovations, clearly require special attention as well as the individual innovations which have been the focus of most innovation research. We therefore define the following four categories of innovation.

INCREMENTAL INNOVATIONS

These occur more or less continuously in any industry or service activity although at differing rates in different industries, depending upon a combination of demand pressures and technological opportunities. These innovations may often occur, not so much as the result of any deliberate research and development activity, but as the outcome of inventions and improvements suggested by engineers and others directly engaged in the production process, or as a result of initiatives and proposals by users. Many empirical studies have confirmed their great importance in improving the efficiency in use of all factors of production, for example, Hollander's *(FRE4)* 1965 study of productivity gains in Du Pont rayon plants or Townsend's *(FRE5)* 1976 study of the Anderton shearer loader in the British coal mining industry.

They are particularly important in the follow-through period after a radical breakthrough in innovation and are frequently associated with the scaling-up of plant and equipment, and quality improvements to products and services for a variety of specific applications. Although their combined effect is extremely important in the growth of productivity, no single incremental innovation has dramatic effects, and they may sometimes pass unnoticed and unrecorded. However, their effects are apparent in the steady growth of productivity which is reflected in input/output tables over time by major changes in the coefficients for the existing array of products and services. The evidence of demand-led inventions and innovations relates primarily to this category and they account for the vast majority of patents. The Japanese experience of reverse engineering, redesign of production systems and workforce involvement in quality improvement clearly provided great scope for this type of innovation in Japanese companies, as shown in the example of the automobile industry.

RADICAL INNOVATIONS

One of the major criticisms of the demand-pull hypothesis *(FRE6)* and of the related 'rational choice' decision making in generating technical change, relates to the origins and early development of those innovations which could hardly be construed as the cumulative addition of small modifications to existing products and processes. For example, there is no way that nuclear reactors could have emerged from incremental improvements to earlier ways of generating electricity or that nylon could have emerged from improvements in natural textile materials. Schumpeter *(FRE7)* pointed out that railways could not emerge from a combination of stage-coaches and maintained that radical innovations, far from being introduced by 'rational' entrepreneurs on the basis of accurate knowledge of 'demand' from consumers, were usually imposed on an initially unreceptive and unwilling market by rather unusual entrepreneurs.

Radical innovations are discontinuous events and in recent times are usually the result of a deliberate research and development activity in enterprises and/or in university and government laboratories. They are unevenly distributed over sectors and over time, but our research did not support the view of Mensch *(FRE8)* that their appearance is concentrated particularly in periods of deep recession *(FRE6)*, in response to the collapse or decline of established markets. But we would agree with Mensch that, whenever they may occur, they are important as the potential springboard for the growth of new markets, or in the case of radical process innovations, such as the oxygen steelmaking process, of big improvements in the cost and quality of existing products.

They may often involve a combined product, process and organis-ational innovation. Over a period of decades a radical innovation — such as nylon or 'the pill' — may have fairly dramatic effects, but their economic impact is relatively small and localised unless a whole cluster of radical innovations are linked together in the rise of entire new industries and services, such as the synthetic materials industry or the semiconductor industry.

Strictly speaking, at a sufficiently disaggregative level, radical innov-ations would constantly require the addition of new rows and columns in an input/output table whereas incremental innovations would simply change the coefficients. But in practical terms, such changes are introduced only in the case of the most important innovations and with long time lags, when their economic impact is already substantial. Evidence of market-led radical innovation is much weaker than in the case of incremental innovation, since by definition usually no estab-lished market exists. Clearly, however, those technologists and sci-entists who are primarily responsible for inventing and developing radical innovations *do* have a potential market in mind and are influenced by social and economic developments. As Carlota Perez puts it: the search is always to turn base metals into gold and not vice versa. Moreover, the evidence compiled from case studies is so strong that those innovators who take a lot of trouble to identify potential users and study their needs are more likely to succeed than those who do not.

CHANGES OF 'TECHNOLOGY SYSTEM'

These are far-reaching changes in technology, affecting one or several branches of the economy, as well as giving rise to entirely new sectors. They are based on a combination of radical and incremental innov-ations, together with organisational innovations affecting more than one or a few firms. Keirstead *(FRE9)* in his exposition of a Schumpeterian theory of economic development, introduced the con-cept of 'constellations' of innovations, which were technically and economically interrelated. An obvious example is the cluster of synthetic materials innovations, petrochemical innovations, innovations in injection moulding and extrusion machinery, and innumerable application innovations for synthetics introduced in the 1930s, 1940s and 1950s *(FRE6)*.

CHANGES IN 'TECHNO-ECONOMIC PARADIGM' ('TECHNOLOGICAL REVOLUTIONS')

Some changes in technology systems are so far reaching in their effects that they have a major influence on the behaviour of the entire economy. These are the 'creative gales of destruction' which are at the heart of Schumpeter's *(FRE7)* theory of long cycles in economic development. The diffusion of steam power and of electric power are obvious examples of such far-reaching transformations. So too, is the combination of innovations associated with the electronic computer. The expression 'techno-economic paradigm' implies a process of economic selection from the range of the technically feasible combinations of innovations, and indeed it takes a relatively long time (a decade or more) for a new paradigm to crystallise and still longer for it to diffuse right through the system. This diffusion involves a complex interplay between technological, economic and political forces which is discussed further below. Here we insist only on the requirement that a new techno-economic paradigm is one that affects the structure and the conditions of production and distribution for almost every branch of the economy. The impulse to the development of a new techno-economic paradigm arises from the perceived constraints on the further development of productivity, profitability, and markets within the existing dominant mode.

Dosi *(FRE10)* has used the expression 'change of technological paradigm' and made comparisons with the analogous approach of Kuhn *(FRE11)* to 'scientific revolutions' and paradigm changes in basic science. In these terms 'incremental innovation' along established technological trajectories may be compared with Kuhn's 'normal science'. Several other authors have also used the expression 'technological paradigm' to connote broadly similar ideas, while Nelson and Winter *(FRE12)* have used the concept of 'generalised natural trajectories' and Sahal *(FRE13)* has developed the idea of generic technologies.

While there are similarities in all these concepts, the approach of Carlota Perez *(FRE14, FRE15)* is the most systematic and has some important distinguishing features. She argues that the development of a new 'techno-economic paradigm' involves a new 'best practice' set of rules and customs for designers, engineers, entrepreneurs and managers, which differ in many important respects from the previously prevailing paradigm. Such technological revolutions give rise to a whole series of rapidly changing production functions for both old and new products. While the exact savings in either labour or capital cannot be precisely foreseen, the general economic and technical advantages to be derived from the application of the new technology in product and process design become increasingly apparent and new rules of thumb are gradually established. Such changes in paradigm make possible a quantum leap in potential productivity, which is at first realised only in a few leading sectors. In other sectors such gains cannot usually be realised without organisational and social changes of a far-reaching character.

The new information technology paradigm, based on a constellation of industries, which are among the fastest growing in all the leading industrial countries, such as computers, electronic components and telecommunications, has already resulted in a drastic fall in costs and a counter-inflationary trend in prices in these sectors, as well as vastly improved technical performance. This combination is relatively rare in the history of technology and it means that this new paradigm satisfies all the requirements for a Schumpeterian revolution in the economy. Our research showed that this technological revolution is now affecting, although very unevenly, all other sectors *(FRE2)* because of its actual or potential economic and technical advantages. In considering this technological revolution, we must take into account not only particular products or processes, but the changes in organisation and structure of both firms and industries, which accompany the introduction of information technology. Several commentators, in emphasising the profound transformation which is involved in large firms (such as General Motors), have described the changes as a 'Cultural Revolution'.

In addition to fundamental changes in the management structures of large firms, and in their procedures and attitudes, there are many other parallel effects of the spread of information technology through the economy: the capability which it confers for more rapid changes in product and process design; the much closer integration of design, production and procurement functions within the firm; the reduced significance of economies of scale based on dedicated capital intensive mass production techniques; the reduction in numbers and weight of mechanical components in many products; the much more integrated networks of component suppliers and assemblers of final products and the related capital-saving potential; the growth of new 'producer services' to supply manufacturing firms with the new software, design, technical information and consultancy which they increasingly require; and the extremely rapid growth of many small new innovative enterprises to supply these services and new types of hardware and components.

Thus, changes of techno-economic paradigm are based on combinations of radical product, process and organisational innovations. They occur relatively seldom (perhaps twice in a century) but when they do occur they necessitate changes in the institutional and social framework, as well as in most enterprises, if their potential is to be fully exploited. They give rise to major changes in the organisational structure of firms, the capital stock, the skill mix and the management style of industry.

The pattern of structural and institutional change

The overwhelming importance of such technological transformations is that, *if* the problems of institutional adaptation and structural change can be overcome, they offer tremendous scope for new employment-generating investment as well as labour-saving productivity gains. These opportunities arise both in the provision of new and improved consumer goods and services and in the provision of a new range of capital equipment for all sectors of the economy.

Although Japanese firms have not been the major contributors to radical innovation in the past, their management style and resources were particularly well suited to the rapid identification and exploitation of this new techno-economic paradigm. The Japanese technological forecasting system did indeed identify the main elements of the emerging information technology paradigm much earlier than elsewhere and this enabled Japanese firms to exploit the potential of the new paradigm in such areas as robotics, CNC machine tools and FMS more rapidly than anyone else. As Carlota Perez has suggested, when a new technological paradigm is clearly unfolding then what would previously have been considered as 'radical' innovations, tend to become 'incremental', since the extension of the trajectory to cover all types of product and process becomes 'common sense' for those who are attuned to the new paradigm.

However, as she points out *(FRE14)*, it is not always easy for companies (or countries) to adapt to a change of paradigm. Indeed she has suggested that depressions represent periods of mismatch between an emerging new paradigm and the old institutional framework. Big boom periods of expansion occur when there is a 'good match' between a new techno-economic paradigm or style and the socio-institutional climate. The widespread generalisation of a new paradigm, not only in the leading branches but also in many other branches of the economy, is possible only after a period of change and adaptation of many social institutions to the potential of the new technology. whereas technological change is often very rapid, there is usually a great deal of inertia in social institutions, buttressed by the political power of established interest groups, as well as by the slow response times of many individuals and groups. The structural crisis of the 1980s is, in this perspective, a prolonged period of social adaptation to this new paradigm. This approach is reminiscent of Marx's theory of tension between the productive forces which have a certain degree of autonomy based on technical change, and production relations which tend to reinforce and preserve existing social arrangements.

Each successive structural crisis raises problems of institutional adaptation, but Perez is not suggesting that socialism is the only possible outcome. On the contrary, socialist economies are confronted with the need for profound institutional changes as are the capitalist societies, a fact increasingly recognised both in the USSR and China.

Perez insists that there is scope for a variety of alternative social and political solutions, which might offer a good match, and sees the present period as one of a social and political 'search for satisfactory solutions'. The outcome will depend on the lucidity, strength and bargaining force of the conflicting social groups and the experience of various countries as they strive for technological and economic leadership and make a variety of institutional experiments and innovations. However, all the potential solutions would be based on the widespread use of information technology throughout the economic system. This assumption seems realistic in the light of the current worldwide diffusion of the new technology, as well as in terms of the general experience of international diffusion of technology over the past two centuries. This experience suggests that the competitive pressures in the world economy are so strong that it is very hard to be 'non-conformist' once a paradigm has crystallised. Technological choices become increasingly constrained, through economies of scale and standardisation of components and machinery, even though an element of social and political choice remains. Socialist countries, which have attempted initially to opt out of a pattern of technology characteristic of the capital countries have, after a decade or so, generally been obliged to fall in line with the worldwide trend, with relatively minor differences. This was the case with the USSR, who after intense controversy in the 1920s adopted Fordist assembly-line technology and even Taylorism in an effort to overtake industrialisation in the capitalist countries. It is apparently now also the case with China, who after a rather more determined attempt to develop and diffuse alternative technological systems, is now falling into line with the general trend of world technology.

The promotion of generic technologies, especially information technology, has become a regular feature of technological policy and industrial policy in almost every member country of the Organisation for Economic Cooperation and Development (OECD) in the course of the 1970s and 1980s. The extent to which such efforts are successful will depend not simply on the scale of resources which are committed in the public and private sectors of the economy, but also on the 'national system of innovation'. The Japanese system seems particularly well adapted to take advantage of the enormous potential of this new paradigm, for several reasons.

1 The systems approach to process and product design.

2 The flexibility of the industrial structure.

3 The capacity to identify crucial areas of future technological advance at national and enterprise level.

4 The capacity to mobilise very large resources of technology and capital in pursuit of strategic priorities.

However, although the Japanese system appears more capable than most others of handling the problems of structural change, the transformation of the skill profile and the capital stock present big problems everywhere.

The skill profile associated with the new techno-economic paradigm appears to change from the concentration on middle-range craft and supervisory skills to increasingly high- and low-range qualifications, and from narrow specialisation to broader multi-purpose basic skills for information handling. Diversity and flexibility at all levels substitute for homogeneity and dedicated systems.

The transformation of the profile of capital equipment is no less radical. Computers are increasingly associated with all types of productive equipment as in Computer Numerical Control (CNC) machine tools, robotics, and process control instruments, as well as with the design process through Computer-aided Design (CAD), and with administrative functions through data processing systems, all of which are linked by data transmission equipment. According to some estimates computer-based capital equipment already accounts for nearly half of all new fixed investment in plant and equipment in the US.

The deep structural problems involved in this change of paradigm are now evident in all parts of the world. Among the manifestations are the acute and persistent shortage of the high-level skills associated with the new paradigm, even in countries with high levels of general unemployment, and the persistent surplus capacity in the older 'smokestack' energy-intensive industries, such as steel, oil and petrochemicals.

As a result there is a growing search for new social and political solutions in such areas as flexible working time, shorter working hours, reeducation and retraining systems, regional policies based on creating conditions for information technology (rather than tax incentives to capital-intensive mass production industries), new financial systems, possible decentralisation of management and government, and access to data banks at all levels. But so far, these seem still to be partial and relatively minor changes. If the Keynesian revolution and the profound transformation of social institutions in World War Two and its aftermath were required to unleash the 4th Kondratiev upswing, then social innovations on a much more significant scale are likely to be needed now. This applies especially to the international dimension of world economic development.

Cross-sector diffusion and differential growth rates of productivity

In describing the advantages of a new techno-economic paradigm, we have stressed the ability to bring about a quantum jump in productivity. However, the *actual* rates of productivity increase have declined since the 1960s in most industrial countries. How is this apparent paradox to be explained?

First of all, it is essential to keep in mind that the new paradigm has been diffusing in a world still dominated by the older energy-intensive mass production paradigm. The symptoms of diminishing returns to the massive investment in this older paradigm were evident in declining capital productivity in most industrial sectors in almost all OECD countries since the late 1960s. But they have also become apparent in the declining rate of increase in labour productivity.

Secondly, in assessing the growing impact of the new techno-economic paradigm, it is necessary to take into account all that has been said above about the problems of structural adjustment, before a good match is achieved between the new paradigm and the institutional framework. This process is very uneven between different countries and different industrial sectors. Therefore, in examining these phenomena it is essential to move to a disaggregated level of analysis, since what we are discussing is the extremely uneven diffusion of a new technological paradigm from a few leading sectors to the economy as a whole.

The TEMPO project at the Science Policy Research Unit (SPRU) attempted to study the long-term changes in labour and capital productivity in the principal sectors of the British economy (the 409 industries distinguished in the Cambridge growth model) from 1948 to 1984. The account which follows is based on five volumes of that analysis and the full summary *(FRE2)*. In our view, although there are important national variations, the broad picture which is described below is characteristic of all the major OECD industrial economies.

When we analyse changes in labour productivity and in capital productivity over the past 20 years at a sufficiently disaggregated level, then we find the following picture:

1   The sectors with the highest rates of growth in labour productivity are the electronic industries, and especially the computer industry and the electronic component industry. These are the industries which make the greatest use of their own technology for design, production, stock control, marketing and management. They are also the only industrial sectors which show a substantial rise in *capital* productivity. They are the sectors which demonstrated the advantages of the new technologies for everyone else and may be described as the 'carrier' and 'motive' branches of the new paradigm.

2   In those sectors which have been heavily penetrated by microelectronics, both in their product and process technology, there is also evidence of a considerable rise in labour productivity and even some advance in capital productivity in the most recent period. This applies, for example, to the scientific instruments industry, to the telecommunications industry and to the watch industry. These sectors have now virtually become a part of the electronics industry.

3   In sectors where microelectronics has been used on an increasing scale over the past 10 years, but where older technologies still predominate in product and process technology, there is a very uneven picture. Some firms have achieved very high productivity increases, some have stagnated, while others actually show a decline in productivity. This is the case, for example, in the printing industry, in the machine building industries and in the clothing industry. This uneven picture is completely consistent with Solter's *(FRE16)* 1960 vision of the spread of new technologies within established industries through new capital investment. In many cases, information technology is introduced in a piecemeal fashion in one department or for one activity and not as part of an integrated system. For example, one or a few CNC machine tools are introduced or a few robots or word processors. These are small

'islands' of automation. This is not yet a computer-integrated manufacturing or office system and does not yet achieve anything approaching
the full potential productivity gains. There may even be a temporary
fall in productivity, because of the lack of the necessary skills in
design, in software, in production engineering, in maintenance and in
management generally. Problems of institutional and social adaptation are extremely important, and flexibility in social response is very
varied between countries, as well as between enterprises. Among
OECD countries, Japan and Sweden appear to have been particularly
successful in making progress in the area of 'mechatronics', but the US,
which has been rather successful in achieving productivity gains in the
microelectronics area (although much less so than Japan), has been
rather unsuccessful in the mechatronics area, with the partial exception of defence-based industries.

4 Sectors producing standardised homogeneous commodities on a flow
   production basis in large plants have made considerable use of
   information technology in their process control systems and in various
   management applications. They were indeed among the earliest users
   of computers for these purposes. This applies, for example, to the
   petrochemical, oil, steel and cement industries. This has helped them
   to achieve considerable improvements in their use of energy and
   materials, but the gains in labour productivity have often been less
   than in the 1950s and 1960s. Capital productivity in these firms usually
   shows a marked decline. To understand this phenomenon, it is
   essential to recognise that these industries are among those most
   heavily affected by the shift from an energy-intensive and materials-
   intensive mass production technological paradigm to an information-
   intensive paradigm. At the height of the consumer durables and
   vehicles consumption boom of the 1950s and 1960s, they were
   achieving strong labour productivity gains based on big plant
   economies of scale. But with the change in the technological paradigm, the slow-down in the world economy, and the rise in energy
   prices in the 1970s, they now often face problems of surplus capacity
   and high unit costs based on below-capacity production levels.

5 Service sectors which are completely based on information technology
   — software services, data banks, computerised information services,
   design services, etc — are among the fastest growing and, for
   individual firms, the most profitable activities in the leading industrial
   countries. But although their growth potential is enormous, they so far
   account for only a small proportion of total services output and
   employment. Productivity statistics are extremely difficult to generate,
   but inferential evidence suggests high rates of growth.

6 Some other service sectors have been considerably affected by information technology, such as banking, insurance and distribution. In these sectors, although the diffusion of new technology is extremely uneven, both by firms and by country, there is evidence of significant gains in labour productivity. This phenomenon is rather important because hitherto it has often been observed that the service sector of the economy was not capable of achieving the type of labour productivity gains achieved in manufacturing. Information technology now offers the potential (and in some cases already the reality) of achieving such gains outside manufacturing. However, the progress of technology depends heavily on institutional and structural changes.

7 In most service sectors, information technology still has diffused only to a small extent, and these areas are still characterised by very low labour productivity gains, or none at all. The stagnation in labour productivity in these sectors may be attributed to the *lack* of information technology, but it certainly cannot be attributed to the impact of information technology. These account for by far the larger part of the tertiary sector.

8 Finally, in many industrialised economies there are sectors which have shown labour productivity gains over the past 10 years, which are due far more to structural rationalisation than to the direct impact of new technology. Examples are the textile and food industries and also the oil, steel, cement and petrochemical industries, where plant closures and rationalisation have been implemented. Since in any industry there is always a 'tail' of low productivity plants, a significant rise in average labour productivity can always be achieved simply as a result of scrapping the older generations of plant, even without any further technical improvements in the more recent plants, which can now work closer to full capacity. This may be described as the 'Verdun' effect in contrast to the 'Verdoorn' effect of the high boom period.

Summing up this discussion, it is not difficult to see that the slowdown in *average* labour productivity gains over the 1970s and 1980s, which has been a worldwide phenomenon in comparison with the 1950s and 1960s, is precisely the aggregate outcome of a structural crisis of adaptation or change of techno-economic paradigm, which has accentuated the uneven development in different sectors of the economy.

On the one hand, the previously dominant energy-intensive mass production paradigm or 'technological regime' was reaching limits of productivity and profitability gains, due to a combination of exhaustion of economies of scale; erosion of profit margins through 'swarming'; market saturation in some sectors; diminishing returns to technical activities (Wolff's Law); and cost pressures on input prices. On the other hand, the new paradigm, which offers the possibility of renewal of productivity gains and increased profitability, has so far deeply affected only a few leading edge industries and services.

The full realisation of the productivity gains which can be achieved as a result of information technology depends on the diffusion of the new paradigm throughout the economy. This in turn will be possible only as a result of many social and institutional changes, which will involve interrelated organisational and technical innovations, as well as a large increase in new skills and a transformation of the existing capital stock.

Conclusions

The structural crisis of the 1970s and 1980s differs in important respects from that of the 1920s and 1930s. In both cases a revolutionary new technology demonstrated its potential for extraordinarily rapid productivity growth, but the problems of social and institutional adaptation to the computer and information technology revolution are very different from those of adaptation to the assembly line and flow production systems of the 1920s.

There is no escape from the study of the specific problems of each new technology. The search for social and institutional adaptation to its peculiar characteristics will dominate the 1980s and 1990s as surely as the Keynesian revolution and the welfare state dominated the 1930s and the 1940s. There is no quick fix in terms of real wage reductions to stimulate labour-intensive techniques. Long-term stable growth depends on post-Keynesian not pre-Keynesian economic policies.

Such institutional changes include the education and training system; the industrial relations systems; managerial and corporate structures; the prevailing management styles; the capital markets and financial system; the pattern of public, private and hybrid investments; the legal and political framework at both regional and national level; and the international framework within which trade and investment flow and technologies diffuse on a worldwide scale.

To bring about such institutional transformation on the requisite scale requires public policies in all these spheres. It cannot occur exclusively in response to private market signals and private market forces. Attempts to return to the pattern of the 19th century are an anachronism. The complexity of advanced industrial economies, the scale of public expenditure and public investment, the long timescale of much of the research, development and infrastructural investment, and the irrelevance of the unaided market mechanisms in many areas are among the reasons why a return to 18th or 19th century prescriptions is a delusion, and could tend to perpetuate large-scale unemployment. What is needed is not pre-Keynesian but post-Keynesian economics. Unfortunately there is not yet evidence of the emergence of an international consensus adequate to cope with the deepening of the structural crisis. For this reason, although there may be room for long-term optimism, the outlook in the short and medium term must be characterised as bleak and the possibility of a more serious depression taken seriously.

References

FRE1
Elster J
Explaining Technical Change
Cambridge University Press
(1983)

FRE2
Freeman C and Soete L L G
Technical Change and Full Employment
Basil Blackwell
(1987)

FRE3
Technological Trends and Employment
Soete L L G (ed)
Electronics and Communications
vol 3
Gower Press Aldershot
(1985)

FRE4
Hollander A G
The Sources of Increased Efficiency: A Study of Du Pont Rayon Plants
MIT Press
(1965)

FRE5
Townsend J F

'Innovation in coal mining machinery: the Anderton Shearer Loader —
the role of the NCB and supply industry in its development'
SPRU Occasional Paper no 3
Univ of Sussex
(1976)

· *FRE6*
Freeman C, Clark J and Soete L L G
Unemployment and Technical Innovation: A Study of Long Waves in
Economic Development
Frances Pinter London
(1982)

FRE7
Schumpeter J A
Business Cycles: A Theoretical, Historical and Statistical Analysis of the
Capitalist Process
2 vols
McGraw-Hill New York
(1939)

FRE8
Mensch G
Das Technologische Patt
Umschau Frankfurt
(1975)
English translation: Stalemate in Technology: Innovations Overcome
Depression
Ballinger New York
(1979)

FRE9
Keirstead B G
The Theory of Economic Change
Toronto
(1948)

FRE10
Dosi G
'Technological paradigms and technological trajectories'
Research Policy
vol 11 no 3
pp 147-163
(1982)

FRE11
Kuhn T
The Structure of Scientific Revolutions
Chicago Univ Press
(1962)

FRE12
Nelson R R and Winter S G
'In search of useful theory of innovation'
Research Policy
vol 6
pp 36-76
(1977)

FRE13
Sahal D
'Technology productivity and industrial structure'
In Technological Forecasting and Social Change
vol 24 no 1
pp 1-15
(1983)

FRE14
Perez C
'Structural change and the assimilation of new technologies in the economic and social system'
Futures
pp 357-375
(Oct 1983)

FRE15
Perez C
'Microelectronics, long waves and world structural change'
World Development
vol 13 no 3
pp 441-463
(1985)

FRE16
Solter W
Productivity and Technical Change
Cambridge University Press
Cambridge
(1960)

SIIT—M

Chris Freeman

Professor Emeritus Freeman works with, and has in the past directed, the Science Policy Research Unit at the University of Sussex. From 1981-84, he studied the problems of technical change and employment; since 1984, he has focused on technological policies, technical innovation and economic theory. His publications are many, including, The Economics of Industrial Innovation (second edition, London, Frances Pinter and MIT Press, 1984) and Information Technology and Employment: an Assessment (Brussels, IBM, 1985).

Subject and contributor index

Subject and contributor index

Subject and Contributor Index